FRESH OUT OF FIRE

Overcoming cancer through faith in
the finished works of Jesus

DR. KEMI TOKAN-LAWAL

WESTBOW
PRESS®
A DIVISION OF THOMAS NELSON
& ZONDERVAN

WestBow Press books may be ordered through booksellers or by contacting:

WestBow Press
A Division of Thomas Nelson & Zondervan
1663 Liberty Drive
Bloomington, IN 47403
www.westbowpress.com
844-714-3454

ISBN: 979-8-3850-2381-3 (sc)
ISBN: 979-8-3850-2383-7 (hc)
ISBN: 979-8-3850-2382-0 (e)

Library of Congress Control Number: 2024907821

Print information available on the last page.

WestBow Press rev. date: 8/19/2024

"To all resilient overcomers,
Treading through stormy seasons of life,
Facing journeys too treacherous to navigate alone…
Lift your gaze to the rock that stands unshaken,
let him carry you…
Look up to the hills my friend, for thence cometh your help.
In those towering peaks, in the darkest moments,
Remember, you are not alone…
Hold on to your faith, that is your anchor.
Faith is the believers' voice of victory!

DR. KTL
…..hiding behind the cross*

CONTENTS

ACKNOWLEDGEMENTS

Thank you; God the Father, God the Son, God the Holy Spirit-The holy trinity. I am thankful for the *substitutional* sacrifice made on the cross of Calvary. Your selfless act has granted me the gift of life. Through your sacrifice on the cross and the guiding presence of the Holy Spirit, I find the strength to journey through life's uncertainties. Because Jesus died, I live!

Eternally grateful for my parents; My Dad, Barrister Olasoji Fayose, of blessed memory, and my mum, Mrs. Remi Fayose, who prays for me endlessly- my chief intercessor, who taught me the importance of prayer. As a little girl, I would tag along to many prayer meetings and conferences, exposing me to the truth of God's word. I am forever grateful that you taught me early to have faith in God!. "Step by Step, needlework!" (Inside joke).

To my darling husband, my lover, the one that I keep looking at his palms for holes…If not that there are no holes in his hands, I would have believed that he is Jesus (inside joke). You are my voice of reasoning, my mentor, my teacher, and my king! The best way to describe you is - "If kindness was a person!" The one God gave me to partner with for purpose. The one God has used to ease my journey. My chairman! Mr. Tokan! Adedolapo Tokan-Lawal. Men like you are rare, uncommon, very few! You remain the best decision I have made after giving my life to Christ. Thank you for being a rock, as wise as a serpent yet as gentle as a dove. I love you and I am forever grateful I get to do life with you!

To my amazing babies, my little soldiers! The ones that walked through the fire with me unfiltered- Tirenioluwa and Tobanimi, like your names depict- you belong to God. It could only have been God who raised you guys and took care of you through that season. Your hugs, your words…, and just looking at you guys every day made me know that God was still writing my story. Indeed, you make the scripture come alive. "And all thy children shall be taught of the LORD, and great shall be the peace of thy children." Isiah 54:13 (KJV). Forever grateful for the gift of you kiddos!

To my younger brother and best friend- Ladipo Fayose. It's amazing how God allowed us to go through wilderness seasons around the same time. It shows how intentional God is about us, our destinies, and our purpose. Surely, coming as siblings was no fluke. It's ordained by God. You and Mum put your phone on standby when I couldn't stand being alone. I had just gotten better, and it seemed like I had died and woken up again. You stayed on video calls with me for hours and helped me navigate life again. I am thankful for family!

To my friends, the ones that walked with me through the difficult season, the ones that God positioned to be there afterward, the ones that had dreams that God was asking them to pray for me, the ones that heard it clearly and started to cover me. Just to mention a few: Woman of Destiny (Est 2001), Moni, Funke Dezarn, Jaye Omokungbe, Toni Philip-Aina, Chukwunonso Eghen, Tope Awodiji, Gbemi Cooper. Your support was immense. An African adage says, "Eniyan laso bora," meaning- "Humans are my clothing." Forever grateful to you guys!

To my sis-in-law, Nike, and her boo Kayode. I am thankful for the gift of you guys. God used you for me in a season where I was extremely vulnerable. He taught me such a huge lesson in the process. You took us into your home, as my entire environment triggered me so much, and I needed to move far away from where I had gone through the wilderness experience. Your home represented rehabilitation mentally, physically, and spiritually for us. You loved on the kids and committed to taking daily walks with me as I was just recovering. I landed at the airport limping such that I was asked if I wanted the ride for old people (lol), but by the time I had hit three months in your home, I could run the Olympics. You are amazing Niks! God bless and reward you!

To Justice Aderonke Harrison (whom we fondly call "Auntiee"), my foundation in Christ as a little girl was from bible club. You invested time, opened your home, and raised us in the word and the fear of God back then in 1004. Thank you, ma, for giving to the lord.

To Architect Jumoke Adenowo, I was only 20 years old when Akin and I visited your office in Onikan. I was a new believer, and that visit marked my life. I saw one who represented Christ with elegance, and I wanted to know her God. From Awesome youth programs in Ife to Awesome treasures meetings in Muson, my story will be incomplete without mentioning the immense impact and difference sitting under your teachings over the years have made in my life. Thank you, ma, for giving to the lord.

To my church families through various seasons-FECA VI, Christ love fellowship, God's love tabernacle, Healing wings chapel of faith, God-chasers & Pastor Lanre-Rex Onasanya. You all contributed to my knowledge of what I know about what was done for us on the cross as believers in Christ Jesus. In this kingdom, what we know matters, because it's the truth that we know that sets us free. Forever grateful that our paths crossed.

To my spiritual fathers, Pastor Segun Obadje (God's love

tabernacle), Pastor Poju Oyemade (Covenant nation), Apostle Joshua Selman (Koinonia global), and Dr Creflo Dollar (Creflo Dollar ministries). I am forever grateful that I have been privileged to sit under your teachings over the years. I am grateful I belong to this spiritual lineage of faith. It is on the foundation of faith that was laid under your tutelage and all you taught me about the kingdom that I was able to fight the good fight of faith when the day of reckoning came. Thank you, sirs, for giving to the Lord.

DEDICATION

To the Holy Trinity, who gave me the privilege of walking this path. You stayed true to your word, which says, "I will never leave you nor forsake you." Hebrews 13:5 (NKJV). Thank you, sir! By the comfort by which I have been comforted by you on this journey, I am dedicated to comforting others.

PREFACE

Going through life's challenging seasons, the inspiration and guidance from those who have trodden a similar path can be found to be a source of strength. Though I had never met him in person, Dr Creflo Dollar, a giant father in the realm of faith, played a pivotal role in my path. He became a ray of hope during my difficult season. I realized the importance of seeking out someone who had faced such a struggle and walked a similar path. This can undoubtedly be a profound source of strength and triumph.

I vividly recall the moment I received the daunting diagnosis. I remembered Dr. Dollars journey, which I was privileged to have stumbled upon on Youtube months before. He spoke about his journey through cancer and the steps he took to navigate this season. I resolved to listen to his message, to meticulously note each step he took, believing that as he had overcome, so would I. With this knowledge, I embarked on my journey, guided by the Holy Spirit.

Our journeys were different, but the principles remained the same. I firmly believe that the Holy Spirit leads us through unique truths in our journeys while grounding us in word principles. It is my prayer that one day, someone will pick up this book and say, "With the principles highlighted in this book, I navigated my hard season through the guidance of the Holy Spirit, and I obtained victory!" I lay bare my scars, so that through *shared* faith and timeless wisdom of kingdom principles, someone can find strength and truth to overcome life's trials, which become a crucible through which Jesus is *revealed* and Christ *glorified*.

INTRODUCTION

HOW TO USE THIS BOOK

Welcome to Fresh out of Fire, overcoming cancer through faith in the finished works of Jesus.

This book is not a mere collection of words. It's a roadmap of principles which will guide our faith journey as you go through life.

To get the most of this book, I recommend using it in conjunction with "Fresh out of fire journal". Available for free download on the websites www.freshoutoffire.com, www.drktl.com, Instagram- @ dr.ktl or in hard copy format. The journal provides space for you to delve deeper after each chapter as you answer the self-introspection questions, which are thought provoking. You get to personalize the principles highlighted to guide your personal journey and curate your own personal declarations and confessions. Through its pages, alongside the book, you tailor your journey with profound wisdom, shaping your path towards victory because *in this kingdom, what you* **know** *matters. It is the truth you* **know** *that will make you free.*

**"And you shall know the truth, and
the truth shall make you free."
John 8.32 (NKJV).**

Rooting for you,
Dr kemi Tokan-Lawal
…. Hiding behind the cross.

I AM NOT BATTLING!

"And he said, listen all you of Judah and
you inhabitants of Jerusalem, and you, king
Jehoshaphat! Thus says the lord to you; Do not
be afraid nor dismayed because of this great
multitude, the BATTLE is not yours, but God's."
2 Chronicles 20:15 (NKJV).

Growing up, we recited Psalm 23 day by day. This was a family routine, just like many parents encouraged their children to do back in the day. It was a simple chapter we committed to memory during our morning devotion, a routine etched into our young lives. My brothers and I knew it word for word, and sometimes recited it in extreme sleep mode, grumbling as we were never spared by my mother. Little did I realize then that this cherished psalm would become my unwavering anchor in the tumultuous journey of life.

As I walked through the darkest valleys in my life's journey, I clung to those words:

"Yea, though I walk through the valley of the shadow of death, I will fear no evil; for you are with me; Your rod and your staff they comfort me."
Psalm 23:4 (NKJV).

They were not just verses anymore; they became my lifeline, my refuge, my strength, and my solace. Through every trial and tribulation, the promises held true.

I lay on the hospital bed three days after a nerve-wracking colonoscopy. This is a procedure done to check the inner lining of the gut. As expected, I was gripped with an overwhelming sense of anxiety while awaiting the results.

To give a bit of context, a quick throwback. For about two years, I had been having strange symptoms. Initially, I had spotted mucous in my poop which I shrugged off as something I had eaten. Then I started to see blood in the loo after using the bathroom. I was self-convinced that it was probably hemorrhoids, but then soon after, these symptoms escalated, and I had this relentless weakness that left me unable to walk long distances. It was as if my energy had abandoned me, and even the simplest of tasks left me drained. Then, I started to lose weight rapidly. Being a naturally slim person, you can imagine what that looked like. Soon after, my hair started to fall off. More insidious were the gut issues: I had a change in stool consistency, and for months, I had constant diarrhea after every meal.

A few days before being hospitalized, I had gone to see my primary care doctor, with presenting complaints of weakness, frequent stooling after every meal, and the presence of mucus in my stool. Dr. Kelly attempted to run some tests, but my veins were elusive. A blood draw was impossible. From the look on her face, I knew she was worried just looking at me. My blood pressure had plummeted to dangerously low levels. She referred me in a hurry to a diagnostic center for urgent blood work.

Three days later, I got a call. "Hello, is this Ms. Kemi?" "Yes," I answered. "This is Dr. Kelly speaking. How are you today?" "I am well, thank you," I replied not sure what to expect. "We got the results for your blood work," her voice was laced with urgency. "Your blood levels are alarmingly low. They are 3, far below the normal range of 11-15. You need to get to the emergency room immediately, as I would not want you to collapse," she said adamantly. There was dead silence on both ends. I summoned up some courage. "Okay, thank you," I replied. "I'd be on my way."

I honestly did not know what to do next. For about five minutes, I was blank. I knew this was an emergency. As a medical doctor, I knew what a blood level of 3 implied. I got to the emergency room, and a series of investigations were ordered immediately, among which was a CT scan. After about two hours, the results were in. The CT scan revealed a *suspicious* mass in my colon, as the Dr. on call put it. It was in my rectum, to be precise. This was a worrisome discovery.

The next step in the quest for answers was a biopsy, which led to the colonoscopy, scoping the inner lining of the gut to get a piece of the tumor, which was later sent to pathology for biopsy. This would help determine whether the mass was benign or malignant. At this point, I was on the edge of my seat, hoping for the best as I awaited the biopsy results.

The clock ticked louder as I found myself confined to a hospital bed. It had been three days, facing an overwhelming fear of the unknown. "This hospital admission marked a significant milestone in my life," I thought. It was my first time in hospital for reasons other than childbirth.

Dr. Smith walked into my room. "How are you today?" He asked in his Italian accent. "I'm very well, thank you," I replied, trying to sound calm. But something about his presence confirmed my deepest fears. He had been eagerly waiting for the results, just as I had, and the gravity of the situation had weighed heavily upon him. With trembling hope, I asked, "Is it malignant?" "Yes, the results are as we thought, we only waited to confirm..." he added. In that pivotal moment, my heart was a whirlwind of contrasting emotions. I felt relief and disbelief....

Relief washed over me like a soothing balm. The last two years had been a tumultuous journey through unexplained symptoms of bloating, peculiarities in my digestive system, weight loss, a dwindling appetite, and the unsettling presence of mucous and blood in my poop. As a doctor, I knew the symptoms I was facing were suggestive, but I had been second-guessing and trying to self-diagnose something mild like irritable bowel syndrome, crohn's disease, and others. But now, this diagnosis brought with it a glimmer of closure.

Yet, disbelief clung to me like a shadow. "How could this be happening to someone who has always had good health?" I thought. If you know me well enough, you would always hear me say that I have known Jehovah Rapha, my healer. Sickness was foreign to me. I rarely took medications and hardly ever had even a simple headache. This was after a supernatural encounter I had with the book 'God's

4

Medicine Bottle' by Derek Prince when I was much younger. It spoke about how the word of God is medicine to our flesh and I took it to heart- literally reading the word like I was taking medicine and embracing it as my remedy whenever I felt unwell. I considered myself an epitome of health. I honestly couldn't recall the last time I had taken ill.

With a spotless medical history, I hadn't taken medications for almost two decades, not even for common ailments. My unwavering belief in God's word as my ultimate source of healing had become second nature.

> **"Therefore, let him who thinks he stands take heed lest he falls."**
> **1 Corinthians 10:12 (NKJV).**

Now I lay in the sterile hospital room, the gravity of the situation washed over me. I gazed at the familiar medical equipment as a patient now, not as a doctor. It was so different. I was devoid of thoughts; It was as if the ground beneath me had shifted, and I was standing at the crossroads of a new reality. I stared at the hospital ceiling, feeling utterly lost and speechless in that defining moment. The television in my private hospital room, almost as if by fate, was somehow tuned to TBN (trinity broadcasting network). As I lay there, the screen illuminated with a scripture:

> **"Many are the afflictions of the righteous, but the LORD delivers him out of them all."**
> **Psalm 34:19 (NKJV).**

Those words resonated deep within my heart, a timely reminder of the unshakable promise of divine deliverance. At the same time, a nurse was standing by the other side of the bed, inserting some medication into my intravenous line. "Life always throws curveballs; this is just one," she muttered. "A lot of people go through this and emerge stronger." she added. I nodded in agreement, still at a loss for words. But then, there was this peace…unusual peace, the peace that the bible talks about:

> *"And the peace of God, which surpasses all understanding, will guard your hearts and minds through Christ Jesus."*
> *Philippians 4:7 (NIV).*

I felt peace, and it defied all explanation. I knew that regardless of the storm, I was held by a power greater than myself. It was a knowing, a profound certainty that I was in God's hands.

> *"And the lord, he is the one who goes before you. He will be with you; He will not leave you nor forsake you; do not fear or be dismayed."*
> *Deuteronomy 31:8 (NKJV).*

The next day, I lay in bed for the entire day. I did not feel like talking to anyone. I did not answer any phone calls. I just lay there, staring into the ceiling, trying to process it all. It indeed felt like an insurmountable challenge. And as the nurse's changed shifts and doctors did their rounds, it just seemed like everything was moving except my world, which stood still.

I am a very private person, and the way it works for me is that I always like to know what God is saying before I make major decisions regarding any situation and before being influenced by others. I would typically wait for God to have his take on decisions before I run it by my husband or a close friend, but this time, I couldn't even hear God. It seemed like he was silent on me. I lay there, still trying to process the news.

The doctor had informed me that the mass was quite substantial. "I cannot attempt surgery yet," he explained. "You need to undergo an MRI (an imaging scan) to determine the extent of cancer, and then we would explore potential treatment options." he added. "I would need the mass to shrink sizably before attempting surgery." he said. I was discharged later that day. And I was referred to proceed with these crucial steps.

It was at that moment that it finally sank in. I had been diagnosed with rectal cancer! Cancer? Cancer! The reality of it hit me hard, so hard… and I knew this was war! I needed to make a decision. I made a resolve in my heart: **I AM NOT BATTLING!!**

"Do not be afraid nor dismayed because of this great multitude, for the battle is not yours, but Gods."
2 Chronicle 20:15b (NKJV).

I know you might be wondering what I meant when I said, "I'm not battling." You see, when it comes to cancer, the common narrative often revolves around the term 'battling.' As medical doctors, we often use the term 'battle' in the context of cancer because we are fully aware of the devastating impact of cancer. It's no joke, and it's not to be taken lightly. People often talk about 'battling cancer' as if it's a war that they can match up to. I hear you saying it's a figurative statement. In my case, I choose to interpret it literally. Battles often require an army, a troop in a warfront not a single individual. "I am not battling, because I am too small," I resolved. Cancer is a David and Goliath situation. There will be no victory except the lord uses the small stone in David's hand to kill the big giant Goliath. I knew the battle can never be mine; It is the Lord's.

"Then all this assembly shall know that the lord does not save with sword and spear; for the battle is the lords, and he will give you into our hands. So it was, when the philistine arose and came and drew near to meet David, that David hurried and ran toward the army to meet the philistine.

Then David put his hand in his bag and took out a stone; and he slung it and struck the Philistine in his forehead, so that the stone sank into his forehead, and fell on his face to the earth."
1 Samuel 17:47-49 (NKJV).

I knew that unless the lord did it, I would lose this one. "It's a big mountain, which on my own, I can never win but I have the one who will battle for me." I resolved.

"Who are you, O great mountain? Before Zerubbabel, you shall become plain!"
Zechariah 4:7a (NKJV).

2000 years ago, Jesus Christ came and sacrificed himself on the cross of calvary. He gave himself as a substitutionary sacrifice. A finished work. He had already won the battle for me. So why should I step onto the battlefield against the fierce adversary? A truth concluded 2000 years ago. The Bible makes it clear that for children of God, healing is like bread. Bread is a staple, a gift that is always available and provided by the heavenly father.

*"Then she came and worshiped him, saying,
"Lord, help me!" But He answered and said, it
is not good to take the children's bread and
throw it to the little dogs. And she said, "Yes,
Lord, yet even the little dogs eat the crumbs
which fall from their master's table. Then Jesus
answered and said to her, "O woman, great is
your faith! Let it be to you as you desire." And
her daughter was healed from that very hour."
Matthew 15:25-28 (NKJV).*

I had this vivid image in my mind's eye. A mental picture of the cross of calvary. I imagined myself on a warfront but hiding… hiding behind the cross, knowing I was too little to battle. The one that died on the cross had already done it all for me, and I chose to take that posture. To take shelter in that truth. "I hide myself behind the cross," I said to myself.

*"But he was wounded for our transgressions,
He was bruised for our iniquities; The
chastisement for our peace was upon him,
and by his stripes we are healed."
Isiah 53:5 (NKJV).*

Although I was not *battling*, I knew that I had to *fight*… I had to fight the good fight of faith, which means to reinforce the finished works of Jesus by having faith in his Gods word in the face of this adversity.

*"Fight the good fight of faith, lay hold on
eternal life, to which you were also called,*

and have confessed the good confession
in the presence of many witnesses."
1 Timothy 6:12 (NKJV).

Having absorbed countless teachings in the church, this was the day of reckoning. It was the moment I had to put into practice everything I had learned. It seemed as though I had been attending classes, and now I had to write an exam.

Principles

1. *Life sometimes throws unexpected curveballs at us. God never promised there would be no afflictions, but he promised that he would deliver us from them all.*
2. *Healing is a finished work; 2000 years ago, Jesus Christ died so you and I may live.*
3. *We stay in good health by grace and mercy, not because of what we have done that we should boast but because of what Jesus did on the cross.*
4. *After receiving negative news like a cancer diagnosis, it's okay not to be okay initially; after all, you are human. But we don't remain that way. We need to make a resolve and remember his grace is sufficient.*
5. *The enemy is not moved by self-pity, depression, or tears. He is moved ONLY by the word of God, so determine your posture.*
6. *When life becomes hard, we are far too small to wage war or fight a battle. Quit battling in your strength; the battle is the lords.*
7. *Healing is available to you; it's a staple for you and I, all God's children.*

8. *Resolve to hide yourself behind the cross and leverage the finished works of Jesus. This is the fight of faith.*

9. *God will never leave you nor forsake you; he is with you even when life's challenges come, no matter the mountains, big or small.*

10. *What you know from the truth about God's word and what you have heard from countless teachings is crucial. The truth you know will set you free.*

Self-introspection Questions

- *In your journal, write about a challenging situation that came as a rude shock. It could be a diagnosis, financial issue, marital issue, a career challenge. Something you never thought would be your life's journey. What's your resolve? Are you wallowing in self-pity, sad and angry at God? What is your heart posture?*
- *What is your honest perspective of challenges? When you face difficult challenges, do you consider yourself a helpless warrior facing a fierce battle? Do you choose to battle on your own or to surrender your battles to the one who has already overcome?*
- *Write down what you truly believe about the finished works of Jesus. Do you believe the singular truth that Jesus already paid the price on our behalf, on the cross of Calvary 2000 years ago? Do you believe he already bore our sicknesses and infirmities? Or do you think you still have to work for it?*

CHAPTER TWO

WHERE AM I LOCATED?

I lay on my bed, knowing that the first step I needed to take was to anchor myself in scripture. I asked myself, "What scripture can I hold onto for this particular situation?" It was then the Holy Spirit brought 'Psalm 91' to my mind. In 2019, just before the pandemic hit and even before I started to have symptoms, the Holy Spirit had given me a specific instruction to meditate upon Psalm 91. The first time I had ever really encountered Psalm 91 was when my spiritual father and Pastor, Apostle Segun Obadje, the set man over God's love Tabernacle global taught us this psalm during bible study for weeks; this was in my final year in university. He broke down this psalm thoroughly, and it marked my life.

In the world of law, there is a document called 'the title deed'. It's a crucial document that is used to assert ownership, particularly when something like landed property is being transferred from one person to another. I will liken this to the kingdom of God. The kingdom of God is a legal system. Where we have title deeds which is the **word of God**. This is how we claim ownership of what God has declared as ours. It is within these promises of God's word that we discover what belongs to us.

As Christians, one of the most important things we can do is to discover what the word of God says in every situation. It is called getting an 'anchor scripture'. A word that one holds steadfastly onto. It's our title deed, our legal claim to what God has promised us. This is applicable in every season of life, and every situation. We have a responsibility to seek out our anchor scripture. We have the word of God as our weapon through which we claim ownership of God's promises and await victory armed with this scripture, what the bible likens to a sword.

"And take the helmet of salvation, and the sword of the spirit, which is the word of God." Ephesians 6:17 (NKJV).

I took the instructions very seriously. My mother and I are close, and I share a lot with her. I shared this instruction I got with her. "Mum, the holy spirit asked me to read Psalm 91 and meditate on it," I said. "Sounds good, I would like to join you on this," she replied. "That would be awesome," I responded. I was glad I had a buddy for the task. We took this powerful passage and meditated on one verse each day; even though I didn't know why then, it was a divine directive. We embarked on the journey to memorizing and meditating on Psalm 91. Our method was one verse daily, internalizing the verse and setting time out to talk about it at the end of the day. It reminded me of the way we memorized Psalm

23 as kids. Through this season, I had fallen in love with Psalm 91 so much that I had studied it in all possible versions of the bible. I attempted to write a devotional based on it as I found it helpful for me especially through the pandemic. I never got around to that, I still may, who knows! But then, little did I know that this scripture would become my anchor during this challenging time.

*"He who dwells in the secret place of the most high
shall abide under the shadow of the Almighty."
Psalm 91:1 (NKJV).*

Another version says,

*"If anyone lives in Almighty God's safe place,
the most high God protects that person."
Psalm 91:1. (Easy version).*

"Kemi, **where are you located?**" I asked myself. "According to Psalm 91 verse 1, I am located, I dwell, in the secret place of the most high, under the shadow of the Almighty. A place called *God's safe place*," I replied to myself. I believed it, that was my title deed, and that settled it. I continued reading and got to verse 5,

*"God will keep you safe, so that no trap will
catch you. He will not let any illness to kill me."
Psalm 91:5 (Easy version).*

I highlighted this as well, I believed it, and that settled it. "He will not allow this diagnosis to kill me!" I read on, and I got to verse 7,

"A thousand people may die near you.
Even ten thousand people may die at
your side. But nothing will hurt you."
Psalm 91:7 (Easy version).

"Kemi, even if the narrative out there is that a lot of people die from this disease, your case is different. Even if you hear the news of ten thousand people dying, it will not come near you," I purposed in my heart. I continued to the last verse,

"With long life, I will satisfy him, and
you will see my salvation."
Psalm 91:16 (NKJV).

Another version says,

"I will give him a long life so that he is happy. He
will see that I have the power to save people."
Psalm 91:16 (Easy version).

That was the verdict "I shall not die but live, the sickness shall not kill me, I'm in God's safe place. I will have a long life to the glory of God. I laid hold on to the promise. This was God's word to me." I declared. I released my faith, I believed it, and that settled it. I had gotten my anchor scripture, which was the word of God to apply directly to this new ordeal and diagnosis I had before me. My title deed for this journey ahead of me.

I went on Youtube and searched up Dr. Creflo Dollars message that he preached at Pastor Andrew Wommack's church. This was a message I had stumbled on months before. Dr. Dollar detailed the steps he took on a journey through cancer. A lot of steps I took through my journey were piggy-backed off Dr. Dollar's testimony.

He taught that he held on to the word and was consistently declaring it over the situation, I went ahead to form my confessions out of my anchor verses. These were my everyday declarations.

> *"And you shall know the truth, and*
> *the truth shall make you free."*
> *John 8:32 (NKJV).*

I learned from one of my fathers of faith Pastor Poju Oyemade of Covenant Nation, that for every challenge we face, it's essential to search out God's word concerning it. The word essentially represents God's judgment over that issue. This was profound and resonated with me deeply. As I mentioned earlier, this felt like I was in an examination room haven to recall the things I had learned in the church over the years. Every situation indeed has a truth, and the Holy Spirit is the one who can guide us into that truth. He illuminates the word, revealing its deeper truths and allocations to our specific situation.

> *"The eyes of your understanding being*
> *enlightened, that you may know what is the*
> *hope of his calling, what are the riches of*
> *the glory of his inheritance in the saints."*
> *Ephesians 1:18 (NKJV).*

One thing is that the Holy Spirit operates in real-time, and we need fresh instructions from him daily, hourly, minute by minute. This is a principle I hold dear. For every season and every situation, we need to ask the lord for the word for that specific situation, more like the specific strategy. What worked yesterday might not work today. It's important to lean in and glean from the Holy Spirit per time.

"Then the Philistines went and made a raid on the valley of Rephaim. And David inquired of God, saying, "Shall I go up against the Philistines? Will you deliver them to my hand?" The Lord said to him, "Go up, for I will deliver them into your hand." So they went up to Baal-Perazim, and David defeated them there. Then David said, "God has broken through my enemies by my hand like a breakthrough of water." Therefore, they called the name of place Baal Perazim. And when they left their gods there, David gave a commandment, and they were burned with fire.

Then, the Philistines once again made a raid on the valley. Therefore, David inquired again of God, and God said to him.

"You shall not go up after them; circle around them and come upon them in front of the mulberry trees. And it shall be when you hear a sound of marching in the tops of the mulberry trees, then you shall go out to battle, for God has gone out before you to strike the Philistines. So David did as God commanded him, and they drove back the army of the philistines from Gibeon as far as Gezer. Then the fame of David went out into all lands, and the lord brought the fear of him upon all nations."
1 Chronicles 14:9-17 (NKJV).

David inquired of the lord for a new *strategy*, even though he was facing the Philistines in battle both times. He inquired of the lord each time and he got a different strategy for overcoming. Same battle, different strategies.

I had profound encounters growing up. I experienced God specifically as Jehovah Rapha, my healer, when I was about 12 years old. It happened that on the first day of every month, I had this strange pattern of migraine headaches. This recurring headache was a mystery to me, but like clockwork, it would arrive, I did not know what to do and would go to the sickbay in high school to get medications. This happened for most of high school, which was about 5 years.

I gave my life to Christ at 17, I decided to pray about this pattern of debilitating migraines, and voila! I received a miraculous healing! This was a turning point in my life. I had experienced God as Jehovah Rapha, my healer. A couple of years later, I was in the university, and I encountered a life-changing book, 'God's Medicine Bottle by Derek Prince'. The book was about a scripture in Proverbs 4:

"My son, give attention to my words; Incline your ear to my sayings. Do not let them depart from your eyes; Keep them in the midst of your heart; For they are life to those who find them, and health to all their flesh."
Proverbs 4:20-22 (NKJV).

This scripture worked for me as it became my anchor for my health for a long time. The revelation I received was that God's word is like medicine for my body, and it works 100% of the time. Whenever I felt unwell, experienced a fever, or sensed any discomfort, I would literally read the word of God, reading it three times a day as if I were taking medication like a prescribed dosage, and without fail. I would get better. This happened time and time again, and I grew to be certain that I was living in the grace of God and the fullness of his healing power.

I can vividly recall a particular moment when I traveled to England for summer vacation. I was enjoying my holidays playing on the swing at a playground with my cousins. We were laughing and talking when suddenly, I felt a wave of nausea and sickness wash over me. Without hesitation, I rushed into the house, grabbed my bible, and began to read it. As I read, I kept confessing that God's word is medicine to my body, and I clung to the truth with all my heart. Miraculously, as I read and confessed, I felt better. It was as though I could physically sense the healing power of Jesus coursing through me. It was a remarkable moment, a testament to the incredible power of God's word. I had developed a deep understanding of Jehovah Rapha, my healer, and I continued to experience his healing power in my life through this scripture.

Years later, I found myself in this new and unexpected season. When the symptoms initially started, and I hadn't visited the hospital yet, I tried so hard to confess and meditate on this *same* word that had always worked, hoping all the funny symptoms would disappear, but nothing changed. For a while, I was perturbed. "What could be wrong?" I wondered. I felt God was ignoring me.

"However, when he, the spirit of truth, has come, he will guide you into ALL TRUTH; for he will not speak on his own authority, but whatever he hears, he will speak and tell you things to come."
John 16:13 (NKJV)

Then, I realized I needed a different strategy. Which could be a different instruction or maybe a different word. I needed to lean on the Holy Spirit to *guide me into the truth* through this different and new season. I stopped feeling discouraged because I did not get an instant miracle from declaring Proverbs 4:22. Instead, I learned to lean into God afresh to hear the specific word for this new season and trial, and he revealed to me the perfect word for the specific situation.

> *"The steadfast love of the lord never ceases; his mercies never come to an end; they are new every morning; great is your faithfulness."*
> **Lamentations 3:22-23 (NKJV)**

Principles

1. *As believers, we need to get an anchor scripture and title deed for every situation or challenge, we go through by the help of the Holy Spirit.*
2. *The word of God can be likened to a sword that we use to fight the good fight of faith.*
3. *We should always remember to inquire of the lord when we face challenges and hard times.*
4. *It is important to seek God's face for the specific strategy for that specific situation.*
5. *The Holy Spirit is our helper; he will always reveal a word which is God's judgement over the specific situation if you ask.*
6. *The anchor scripture is the sword of truth; we put it to work by declaring and confessing it.*
7. *What worked yesterday may not work today; we need not be discouraged. Be encouraged, knowing there is new wisdom for today's challenge.*
8. *The Holy Spirit was sent to help us navigate tough seasons, and he guides us into ALL truth, not SOME truth.*

9. *We need to leverage on the Holy Spirit in real-time, daily, hourly, minute by minute to guide and lead us.*

10. *We must lean into God to reveal his word and truth to us, building up our Christian faith.*

Self-introspection Questions

- *Search out scriptures that speak to every area of your life (marriage, finances, health, career, etc.). Lean into the Holy Spirit to give you the specific scripture to hold on to for these areas and write them in your journal.*

- *Take time to fellowship with God and inquire of him for the strategy or word concerning any aspect of your life. Write down these new instructions and steps to take in obedience.*

- *Write down the steps you can take daily to help you prioritize your study of God's word, prayer time and to foster intimacy with the Holy Spirit above all other things that demand your attention daily.*

CHAPTER THREE

FEAR CONTAMINATES FAITH

"Yea, Though I walk through the valley of the
shadow of death, I will FEAR no evil; For you are with
me; your rod and your staff, they comfort me."
Psalm 23:4 (NKJV).

I walked into the doctor's office. This was my first visit to Dr. Smith's clinic after being discharged from the hospital. As expected, a few other patients were in the waiting area as well waiting for their appointment with him. While waiting, the ladies who seemed to be familiar with one another engaged in small talk. "My cancer has been for six months," a lady said. "Oh! mine just came back," another replied. The conversation went on. Although I was not interested in any conversations, something struck me. How do they keep referring to it as 'my cancer'? How is this thing yours? I thought. How were they confidently confessing and claiming that it was theirs? "It can never be mine. I will never call this thing mine. I said to myself. It is simply the diagnosis," I resolved.

I have been taught that 'we have what we say'. So, I am generally very particular about the words I use and I do not accept just any labels. I couldn't understand how these ladies could take ownership of something so destructive like cancer. Then again, that's my personal perspective. Unwavering in my conviction, "It's not mine, I'm only passing through," I said to myself. I may be on the journey, but it doesn't make it mine. These were my thoughts and standpoint.

I refused to give it *life*, I was determined not to allow it to take root in my identity, and I staunchly refused the label 'my cancer or my illness'. This was a crucial strategy for me to maintain a positive outlook and avoid negative projections. This worked for me. I needed to protect my mind and mental health, and most importantly avoid fear.

"Death and life are in the power of the tongue, and those who love it and indulge it will eat its fruit and bear the consequences of their words." Proverbs 18:21 (Amplified version).

To show how intentional I was about not calling the name or giving life to the diagnosis, when I turned a corner and started to feel better and was now able to share with my close family and friends, I would still describe it as "that thing that kills people," and they will immediately get it. I was determined not to use my mouth to give life to anything negative. Then again, that was my personal approach given that I understand what works for me. It might not be the same for everyone. The truth is fear contaminates faith. I made up my mind not to allow fear at all costs.

"For God has not given us a spirit of fear, but of power and of love and of a sound mind."
2 Timothy 1:7 (NKJV).

Dr. Creflo Dollar, in his message 'Manifesting healing,' emphasized the importance of always using the right words knowing that words can chart the entire course of the journey. "When I first got the diagnosis, I initially kept it to myself, taking time to process my thoughts and ensuring I had the right words to convey the situation without speaking harmful words," Dr. Dollar said.

Nobody knew what was going on as I had learned over the years not to say anything till I get the right words to say, so as not to say anything that will jeopardize or harm me." he added.

Recognizing this, I made a conscious decision to limit the number of people I shared the diagnosis with, not because they were unkind but because their love for me might lead them to project their fears onto the situation. It's common for people to react to a cancer diagnosis with fear and dread, which was something I needed to avoid for my well-being.

"But when he saw that the wind was boisterous, he was afraid, and beginning to sink, he cried out, saying. "Lord save me!"
Matthew 14:30 (NKJV).

While Peter was centered on God, he walked on water, he was laser-focused regardless of the winds and storms, which can represent the issues and challenges of life, but as he considered the stormy situation, he began to sink. What we focus on matters. It's either we focus on God or choose to focus on the storm. This determines if we will walk on water or we will sink. I was very intentional about the company I kept. I could not afford anything or anyone that would make me consider the storm, as that would mean sinking.

Fear contaminates Faith. Fear is very subtle. The way it creeps in can be so gentle. Often through our thoughts, words, then actions. A great leader once said, "Fear is a spirit that stands at the door. It opens the door for other negative spirits such as death, and destruction."

Having gotten my anchor scriptures, I knew I had to intentionally keep fear at bay. I knew that I needed to avoid fear like a plague, and one of the ways was to guard all my gates: my eyes (what I saw), my thoughts(which are formed by what I see and hear), my ears(what I heard) and my mouth(what I said). I knew this was as important as having the word of faith. God's word says that fear is not of God. Therefore, the spirits of *fear* and *faith* cannot coexist.

I've always known that one of the triggers for fear in my life is the reactions and projections of others. While in medical school, whenever I faced a challenging exam or workload, I would manage it calmly when working in isolation. However, the moment someone expressed anxiety or fear about the situation, I would become anxious. This shift in focus would hinder my progress, and I often struggled to perform at my best. Knowing this, I took some intentional steps such as keeping away from some friends. One of my close friends, who had experienced the loss of family members due to a similar diagnosis, knowing the potential for her to trigger me or sow seeds of her past experiences or even scare her, I made the difficult decision to create some distance. I even went so far as becoming incommunicado to some friends not because they wronged me but because I understood the necessity of maintaining my internal peace and boundaries at this time. Thankfully, they understood when I explained to them the reasons for my actions when I got better. Also, my mother, who is a fervent intercessor-while I greatly trust in her covering- I knew that this was something she might not be able to handle. The news will cripple her with fear. To protect myself from any projected fear, I refrained from sharing the details with her. I provided only a vague description, assuring her that I was well and requesting her continued prayers without exposing her to fear that might affect her prayers.

My husband was extremely helpful. Such a pillar of strength during this challenging time. He never let it become a heavy topic. We never dwelled on it. He treated it like a normal challenge we could face together, focusing on treatment and our plans for the future. He never called the name of the diagnosis either. At some point, I thought he didn't even know. But of course, he did. His calm and supportive presence made a huge difference, preventing fear from taking over our lives.

Also, the friends around me that season were awesome. Even if they suspected, it was never a topic of discussion. This helped me. One of my girlfriends, we would talk often and engage in everyday conversations about God, church, fashion, kids, work, family just general conversations, diverting our thoughts away from fear. She knew what was wrong but chose to be a positive force, which was incredibly helpful. Some other friends prayed for me; they did not pry into the details but simply covered and carried me in prayers, it was a comforting presence through the tough time. To be honest, having the right set of people was important as they fueled my *faith*, not *fear*.

Taking the path of calmness, focusing on maintaining a peaceful and serene mindset, regardless of the turbulence surrounding my situation. This strategy served me well, ensuring that I didn't succumb to fear, and allowing me to navigate my journey with grace and faith. I couldn't afford to let fear take root in my journey.

Finally, I made a conscious effort to guard what I read and surround myself with positivity, especially about stories I read on the internet and social media. Luckily, I stumbled upon a particular lady on Instagram who inspired and helped me. She had triumphed over a similar diagnosis focusing on the power of positive affirmations. She talked about speaking to her body before treatment and telling her cells that they respond well and speaking healing and life to her body by faith. She became my virtual best friend as her journey and mindset resonated with me and helped strengthen my faith.

The truth is what works for one person may not work for another. Some may draw strength from sharing their challenges with family and friends while others, like me, find solace in isolation, positivity and faith. It all depends on what helps you navigate the unique journey you are on. Just remember that in every situation, steer clear of anything that fuels *fear* and embrace what nurtures your *faith* because **fear** contaminates **faith**. And your *faith* is your victory.

> *"For whatever is born of God overcomes*
> *the world. And this is the victory that has*
> *overcome the world -our faith."*
> *1 John 5:4 (NKJV).*

A state of being fearless is a place of rest. Resting in the finished work of Jesus. The idea of operating from a place of rest is crucial. This is something I also picked from Dr. Creflo Dollar's message. He emphasized that we don't need to toil in fear and anxiety; the only labor we are called to is to labor to enter our rest. I found this to be a life-changing perspective. He stated that because we know that healing is a done deal, being able to rest in that reality that is the highest level of faith. I learned to labor into my rest. When a negative thought came to mind, I would combat it with God's word and that settled it, declaring it over and over and over, taking the negative thoughts captive that was the only labor required of me.

> *"For the weapons of our warfare are not carnal but mighty in God for pulling down strongholds, casting down arguments and every high thing that exalts itself against the knowledge of God, bringing every thought into captivity to the obedience of Christ."*
> *2 Corinthians 10:4-5 (NKJV).*

> *"Therefore, since a promise remains of entering his rest, let us fear lest any of you seem to have come short of it. For indeed the gospel was preached to us as well as to them; but the word which they heard did not profit them, not being mixed with faith in those who heard it, for we who have believed do enter that rest, as he said; so I swore in my wrath, they shall not enter my rest although the works were finished from the foundation of the world. For he has spoken in a certain place of the seventh day in this way – and God rested on the seventh day from all his works, let us, therefore, be diligent to enter that rest, lest anyone fall according to the same example of disobedience."*
> *Hebrews 4: 1, 2, 3 & 11 (NKJV).*

This scripture encapsulates the essence of rest. It reminds us that as Christians we have the privilege of entering God's rest; this rest is not a passive state but an active one, where we trust in God's promises and find peace even in the midst of life's storms. A great father of faith, Watchman Nee said, "The Christian life from start to finish is based upon this principle of utter dependence upon the Lord Jesus. There is no limit to the grace God is willing to bestow upon us. He will give us everything, but we can receive none of it except as we rest in him."

I chose *faith* over *fear*.

Principles

1. *You do not have to accept any negative label as yours. Whatever the challenge, you can avoid personalizing it, that doesn't mean denying it, just refuse to give it life with your words because you have what you say.*
2. *Fear is very subtle in its entry; you need to do your part by guarding your heart diligently. The voices you are listening to are crucial, choose the voice of the lord over the doctor's report.*
3. *Guarding your heart may look like being careful and intentional about who you let in and who you leave out during a crisis.*
4. *If you draw strength from others, make sure you surround yourself with people that will fuel your faith, not fear.*
5. *Guard your thoughts; Think about things that are true and of good report. Focus on your victorious outcome from the challenge. Stay positive.*
6. *Guard your gates; eyes, ears, mouth, – what you hear, see, and speak.*
7. *Fear versus faith, whatever you feed grows.*
8. *It's better to say nothing till you have the right words to say than to speak words that will cause harm to you.*

9. *Labor to enter into rest; choose to operate intentionally from a place of rest.*

10. *To enter rest you may have to combat negative thoughts over and over again with God's word, intentionally casting down imaginations to the obedience of God's word.*

Self-introspection Questions

- *Take time to write in your journal a sincere letter to God about the secret areas of your life shrouded in fear. It could be fear of failure, rejection, or fear of the unknown.*

- *Are you intentional about surrounding yourself with individuals who uplift and inspire, who feed your faith rather than fear? Identify and write down what you are feeding your gates – your eyes, ears, and thoughts. What are you reading, listening to and thinking about in this season?*

- *Write down the steps you are taking to confront your fears. What steps are you taking to replace all fears with faith? What are you doing purposefully to help you function from a victory vantage point in every area of your life?*

CHAPTER FOUR

WHEN GOD ALLOWS MOUNTAINS

"Big mountain, you are no problem. You will become
flat ground in front of Zerubbabel. Then he will
bring out the last and biggest stone of my house.
The people will shout, God bless it! God bless it!"
Zechariah 4:7 (Easy version).

This was a huge mountain before me, and I knew it. There was no doubt. I went through all the emotions. At some point, I was in a vulnerable phase. I felt very human. "Why am I facing this? Was this because of my choices?" I wondered. I had no answers. God was silent in that season but there was one profound thing. His presence. It was constant. For so many years, one of the ways God has spoken to me is with numbers. It's like an inner language unique to me. Over the years, I have interpreted it to mean God is with me. In this

31

season, though God's silence was very loud, one thing was constant: the numbers. I always saw the numbers. This reassured me. Also, I was so sure of his love for me, I never doubted it. I was sure then, just as I am now. Never did I for one day doubt it. I was sure of his unending love for me.

"For I am persuaded that neither death, nor life, nor angels, nor principalities, nor powers, nor things present, nor things to come, nor height, nor depth, nor any other, nor any other created thing, shall be able to separate us from the love of God which is In Christ Jesus, our lord."
Romans 8:38&39 (NKJV).

Dr. Creflo Dollar, in his thanksgiving video on Youtube titled 'Greatest Power' answered specific questions about his journey through cancer, one question was "Does God make us sick? Does he put illness on people?" "No, He does not," he responded. This was very profound and it's important to establish that. This means God wants us well. He wishes for his children to prosper in health.

"Beloved, I pray that you may prosper in all things and be in health, even as your soul prospers."
3 John 1: 2 (NKJV).

Dr. Creflo Dollar also mentioned that "There is this myth that when Christians are going through challenges they must have sinned, sometimes Christians are made to feel it's a bad thing to have any reason to go to the hospital," he added. This resonated with me. People imply that the hard seasons that Christians go through, such as illness, financial trouble, marital issues, infertility whatever represents a mountain are because of God's anger. This is not always true.

> *"Now, as Jesus passed by, He saw a man who was blind from birth. And his disciples asked him, saying, "Rabbi, who sinned, this man or his parents, that he was born blind?" Jesus answered, "Neither this man nor his parents sinned, but that the works of God should be revealed in him."*
> *John 9:1-3 (NKJV).*

The Holy Spirit reminded me of the story of the blind man whose eyes had not functioned properly since birth. He had never seen from birth. His condition carried a burden of shame, with questions about his innocence or his parents' sins haunting him. Jesus reframed the situation. He made it clear that the man's condition wasn't punishment but an opportunity to display God's glory. The blind man must have heard a lot of people, including family and friends ask the same question. He may have felt he was a victim of grave injustices. He could have felt that the blindness was his fault. And this would lead to condemnation.

> *"There is therefore now no condemnation to those who are in Christ Jesus, who do not walk according to the flesh, but according to the spirit."*
> *Romans 8:1 (NKJV).*

But Jesus corrected the narrative before he proceeded to give this man sight. It was an opportunity for God's power, glory, and goodness to be showcased, and it continues to shift the paradigm of our perception today. One thing stands true nothing can happen without God's consent, God was aware of the fire when the three

Hebrew men, Shadrach, Meshach, and Abednego were thrown in, and he showed up, he was the fourth man in the fire. God was aware when Daniel was thrown into the lion's den, he showed up, and the lion did not harm him. His grace was sufficient. God was the one that drew the enemy's attention to Job. Nothing happens without his consent.

> *"Now there was a day when the sons of God came to present themselves before the lord, and Satan also came among them, and the lord said to Satan, from where do you come? So Satan answered the Lord and said, "From going to and fro on the earth, and from walking back and forth on it. Then the lord said to Satan, Have you considered my servant job, that there is none like him on earth, a blameless and upright man, one who fears God and shuns evil. So, Satan answered the Lord and said, "Does Job fear God for nothing? Have you not made a hedge around him? Around his household and all that he has on every side. You have blessed the work of his hands, and his possessions have increased in the land, but now stretch out your hands and touch all that he has, and he will surely curse you to your face!" And the Lord said to Satan, Behold all that he has is in your power; only do not lay a hand on his person". So Satan went out from the presence of the lord."*
> *Job 1:6-12 (NKJV).*

God can allow *mountains*. But most importantly, beyond and regardless of the *why, what,* and *how* of the mountain - whatever the mountain represents, as it looks different for everyone-these are variables. The one constant thing is what we **do** to the mountain. What we are meant to do with mountains is to *speak* to them, not to talk about it, wander about it, discuss about it, or think about it. We speak to it! Unfortunately, mountains don't respond or are not moved by tears, pity parties, being depressed, condemned, or even sadness; they only respond to the spoken word of God.

> *"For assuredly, I say to you, whoever says to this mountain, be removed and be cast into the sea, and does not doubt in his heart but believes that those things he says will be done, he will have whatever he says."*
> *Mark 11:23 (NKJV).*

It is our faith that moves mountains. Faith is a currency that we spend in the kingdom, so we need to have faith, believe, and speak to it. The truth is, for a while, it felt like nothing was happening. I kept speaking, confessing, and declaring the word.

There is, therefore, no need to focus on irrelevances and unnecessary narratives. This is *minor,* but we need to focus on God's word and speak the word of God by faith to the situation. We must keep speaking it till we see the change we desire. This is *major*: calling those things that are not as though they are.

> *"As it is written, I have made you a father of many nations. In the presence of him whom he believed- God, who gives life to the dead and calls those things that do not exist as though they did."*
> *Romans 4:17 (NKJV).*

Our focus should remain on the greatest power, no matter what the mountain looks like. God's grace is sufficient.

DR. KEMI TOKAN-LAWAL

*"And he said to me -My grace is sufficient for you,
for my strength is made perfect in weakness."
2 Corinthians 12:9 (NKJV).*

Principles

1. *The presence of a mountain does not signify the absence of God's love for you.*
2. *God's love is unwavering; nothing will separate you from the love of God.*
3. *Nothing can happen in your life without God's consent.*
4. *No matter the mountain, big or small, it is made plain, and the name of the Lord will be exalted and glorified.*
5. *The origin, the complexities, the why's and the how's of the mountains and challenges you are facing are not as important as the actions to take. Which simply put, is to **speak** to it!*
6. *Mountains are not moved by fear, depression, sadness, or pity parties; they are moved by the word of God! By our faith.*
7. *It is your responsibility to speak to the mountain, not God's responsibility.*
8. *Faith in the finished works of Jesus is the currency we spend in the kingdom.*
9. *God's grace is sufficient for you, no matter what the mountain looks like.*
10. *Choose God's narrative above all, and ensure your identity is rooted in Christ.*

36

Self-introspection Questions

- *How do you perceive God's love for you? Do you believe it is unconditional, regardless of the challenges you face? Do you allow the opinions and interpretations of others to influence your understanding of your journey or the reasons behind your challenges?*

- *Write down in your journal some faith declarations for all areas of your life, such as relationships, career, health, finance, and spiritual growth; declaring that in Christ Jesus you are more than a conqueror.*

- *Write down steps you are taking to respond to tough challenges or mountains. Are you allowing yourself to be overwhelmed with tears or depression? Or are you speaking the word of God to the situation?*

CHAPTER FIVE

MODERN MEDICINE IS NOT MUTUALLY EXCLUSIVE TO THE POWER OF GOD

A brief throwback to a time right before I was hospitalized:

One morning, my daughter came to my bedside crying, "What's wrong?" I asked, "Mum, I had a dream," she said. "What was it about?" I inquired. Sobbing seriously amidst tears, she said, "I dreamt that you have cancer." I froze. "Really?" I asked. Quite shocked to be honest; we never talk about stuff like that, I had never even mentioned that *name*. So, I didn't know how she even knew that. She kept sobbing. "Don't worry, dear. The devil is just trying to scare you," I comforted her. "I am well, okay?" I wiped her teary face and got her ready for school. I tried to shrug it off, but I knew in my heart that God had sent this child to me.

"Out of the mouth of babes and nursing infants, you have ordained strength, because of your enemies, that you may silence the enemy and the avenger."
Psalm 8:2 (NKJV).

To be honest, I didn't want to go to the hospital or to seek professional help. How ironic! Given that I am a medical doctor. I know, right! But sincerely, I did not want to go into the hospital. I wanted the healing power of God to heal me in my own way without modern medicine. In retrospect, the truth is that deep down, I had a gut feeling that something was wrong, the symptoms were suggestive, and I knew I needed professional intervention even though I did not want it that way.

A quick throwback to medical school: I had to go through a surgery posting in my fourth year, I was given a presentation topic that was chosen randomly for all students by the lecturer. I had to study extensively and later present it to the entire class. My topic was colorectal cancer, which later became the diagnosis. I studied for my presentation so hard, that I could not miss the symptoms and signs to look out for in such a condition. Fast forward to 14 years later. When I started to have symptoms, I knew in my heart that what I was feeling was just how colorectal cancer presents, even though I denied it. Hence, the reluctance to go to the hospital. I was disturbed, but I tried hard to explain it away. "As doctors, we tend to go extreme and expect the worst diagnosis, probably due to too much knowledge," I thought. I settled for diagnosing myself with milder gut conditions like irritable bowel syndrome or Crohn's disease with the help of Dr. Google(lol).

A few days after my daughter had the dream, my husband got quite adamant, and he insisted that I had to go into the hospital to get checked. He knocked out all the excuses I was making. It's safe to say, "He saved my life!" At this point, I knew I had no choice. This was what led me to go into the primary care doctor's office, which led to unraveling the diagnosis.

It turned out to be stage three rectal cancer. I had been helped by God. Sometimes, God nudges us to seek help in various ways, but we have it planned out the way we want him to answer. Another factor is overthinking the situation which would make it a mental hurdle. I have learned that it's better to obey the Holy Spirit promptly in every situation. In my case, he had nudged me in various ways to go to the hospital. It's always better to obey and face the uncertainty because the enemy thrives in fear of the unknown.

> *"There is no fear in love, but perfect love casts out fear because fear involves torment. But he who fears has not been made perfect in love."*
> *1 John 4:18 (NKJV)*

I was in the bathroom on a random day when treatment was about to start when the Holy Spirit said to me, **"Modern medicine and the power of God are not mutually exclusive."** According to Webster's dictionary, mutually exclusive means that one will automatically rule out the other. It means they can't both be true; one has to exclude the other. But when you say it is NOT mutually exclusive, it means that they can both be true, they can work side by side, and they can happen simultaneously. This was profound it was clear he had heard my thoughts and knew how I was struggling with the place of modern medicine as it relates to the power of God and the healing of a believer. Apostle Joshua Selman, a great father of faith, also said something profound in one of his messages: that for modern medicine to work on the human body is a miracle in itself, and wisdom is profitable to direct.

"God cannot be boxed. He chooses how he will do it," my husband explained. He could choose to heal anyhow, either by a healing miracle or by modern medicine.

I started chemotherapy treatment. Walking into the first treatment session got me very emotional. "God, how can this be my journey?" I thought. I walked into the chemotherapy lounge. It was an entirely different world. Good health is indeed underrated. It was a big space with massage chairs arranged like a living room, so everyone sat facing one another. The entire room was filled with elderly people, grandpas and grandmas. "I do not fit in here," I thought. "Lord, how is this happening to me?" I cried. Statistically, this variant called colorectal cancer is seen more in the elderly. So much so that even the healthcare nurses I met had made comments like, "You are so young!" I had no words.

"The plan is you are going to be on chemotherapy for four months, which is six cycles," Dr. Bally, the oncologist, said. "The way it works is that a port will be inserted in your chest via a minor surgical procedure. Treatment will be infused weekly through the port," he explained. After the chemotherapy, another scan will be done to see how much the tumor has shrunk, after which we will determine the next line of treatment. I cried so hard after hearing this, as four months seemed like forever. I was encouraged when Dr. Bally said, "Just take it like you are sacrificing six months. Let's go ahead and cure this thing." That statement encouraged me. "Well, if this is what it will take, at least there is an end," I thought.

"For surely there is an end, and the expectation
of the righteous shall not be cut short."
Proverbs 23:18 (KJV).

The treatment journey was amidst tears. I had to go in every two weeks for treatment and every other week for blood transfusion, which meant I went in weekly. The grueling sessions brought harsh side effects like diarrhea, loss of appetite, weakness and weight loss. It was tough. The way the treatment was structured was such that I had to stay in the hospital for chemotherapy for three hours and then take the treatment home through the port on my chest for forty-eight hours. At this point, I had taken off my doctor's hat. I was now in the shoes of a patient. For the first time in my life, I felt the pain of patients. This was no longer the books and white coat; It was reality.

Four months down the line, after going through the required treatment cycles, I was scheduled for a repeat scan. I was so excited as I awaited the result. Very optimistic. Lo and behold, a rude shock! "The result came back showing that the tumor had shown no signs of shrinking." Dr. Bally said nervously, "I would be referring you back to the surgeon, Dr. Smith," he added.

My appointment with Dr. Smith was a true test of my faith. He started by stating that he did not think anything would work if chemotherapy did not work. He went on about a lot of negative stuff and prognosis. He referred me back to Dr. Bally, saying that he would go with whatever he decided to do with me.

I stayed calm. I knew I had only one choice, which was to activate my faith. "I need to put pressure on the word, placing a demand on the finished work of Jesus while maintaining my position, hiding behind the cross," I said to myself. I intentionally shrugged off all the negative words he spoke. It was a very conscious effort. "Whose report would you believe?" I asked myself. "I shall believe the report of the lord," I replied. I made up my mind that it doesn't matter what is coming up in the middle of this journey; I choose to focus on the outcome, which is the end: I am healed! It is a done deal! I know the outcome of this journey: I am healed! This happened 2000 years ago! It's already done! It's a finished work!

"Let us hold fast to the confession of our hope without wavering, for he who promised is faithful."
Hebrews 10:23 (NKJV).

I intentionally did not dwell on Dr. Smith's words. Instead, that night I activated JOY!. I rejoiced! Praise is a weapon. I threw myself a very lovely dinner alone. I went into my favorite Jamaican restaurant, ordered a sumptuous meal, and ate it with joy. I was determined to stay in a place of rest. I kept my focus on the finished work of Jesus. Then I kept saying, "Whose report would you believe? I will believe the report of the lord," I declared. This kept my faith activated. I could not afford to allow this news usher in fear neither could I let the feeling of hopelessness and helplessness surface. I had my anchor scripture. I reminded myself of where I was located: I was hiding behind the cross, under the shadow of the Almighty. I know that this sickness will not kill me, and with long life has satisfied me.

"Certainly not! Indeed, let God be true but every man a liar."
Romans 3:4a (NKJV).

"We need to do something for you, we can't just leave you like this," Dr. Bally said at the next appointment. "There is this new line of treatment which we don't use at this stage as a second line of treatment, but I want to use it for you, I will have to break protocol." "It's very expensive but we would use it," he added. As a Dr. with

43

a health insurance background, I doubted. "Would they approve it?" I asked, knowing that new drugs like these run into hundreds of thousands of dollar bills. It was very costly. The hospital had a lot of back and forth with the insurance company but thankfully it was later approved. This time, the treatment structure was different. The port had been removed from my chest. I had an appointment every three weeks for just thirty minutes and through a regular intravenous infusion. "After a few treatments, we will know if this will work. I'm praying for you." Dr. Bally said.

God DID move through modern medicine, and my faith enabled it. By the second dose of immunotherapy (a treatment targeting the immune system), there was a shift. The tumor started to shrink, and I experienced a reversal of symptoms for the first time in three years. Whew! This seemed like David using a very small stone to kill Goliath. I would say without a doubt that life is spiritual. God can use modern medicine, and it is important to back it up with prayers and faith. It is still by his grace and mercy that modern medicine will work, and the body will respond to it. I saw this from my experience with chemotherapy treatment not working. I had a change of perspective. I felt the shift, realizing that life's journey is both physical and spiritual, and for immunotherapy to have worked is through God's mercy. It is God who gives Medical doctors the wisdom for cutting-edge health interventions. Indeed, modern medicine and the power of God are not mutually exclusive. It can happen side by side.

You will wonder how a doctor will avoid hospital-related things. A popular saying goes that 'Doctors are the worst patients.' I can testify to that. I believed more in the power of God than in modern medicine. I often wondered why pastors went to the hospital. But of course, I know better now and I am an advocate of getting checked early because the torture from fear is not even worth it. When what is wrong is detected, then you will know what to pray about specifically.

While healing miracles and divine health are very possible and God is still in the business of doing great miracles which happen every single day!. Apostle Joshua Selman puts it this way in one of his messages: 'There is a place for divine health and miracles, but the things of the spirit take mastery which occurs over time. While we are growing in our faith, we must apply wisdom and be obedient to the spirit of God. And let him work however he chooses. God is the one that gives wisdom to medical professionals, and even the medications are made through his wisdom.'

The truth is, this was quite a grey area for me. I was fine treating patients and diagnosing according to my wealth of medical knowledge, but somewhere in my heart, I did not think much of it. In my unique case, God wanted me to seek professional help.

"He went a little farther and fell on
his face, and prayed, saying,
"O My father, if it is possible, let this cup pass from
Me; nevertheless, not as I will, but as you will."
Matthew 26:39. (NKJV)

Though everyone's journey through challenges may look different. The *mountain* you are facing may look different, it could be finance, marriage, or career. Though the challenges are different, the principle of faith remains the same. We need to activate our faith and choose to hold on steadfast to the promise without wavering. Focusing on the end. For he who has promised is faithful.

45

"But let him ask in faith, with no doubting, for he who doubts is like a wave of the sea driven and tossed by the wind. For let not that man suppose that he will receive anything from the lord. He is a double-minded man, unstable in all his ways."
James 1:6-8 (NKJV).

Principles

1. *Oftentimes, God communicates with us through the simplest ways, and it's important to be discerning.*
2. *We are not to go to God set in our ways but to inquire of his way.*
3. *Seeking professional help does not mean you do not have faith.*
4. *God cannot be boxed; in his sovereignty, he chooses the way he does things.*
5. *Sometimes we do not want to go through the journey, but his grace is sufficient to carry us through.*
6. *Do not respond based on what you hear or see but based on what God's word says.*
7. *Be firmly rooted in God's word and operate from a place of rest, even when things are contrary hold fast to faith.*
8. *Modern medicines and interventions are God's wisdom through man.*
9. *Continually choose to believe the report of the lord over any negative report and rejoice by faith.*
10. *No matter how bleak the situation may seem, be laser-focused on the end, the outcome which is victory. This was already determined by the finished works of Jesus 2000 years ago.*

Self-introspection Questions

- *Pen down in your journal the gentle nudges of the Holy Spirit in any area of your life that you may have been ignoring.*

- *Have you been obedient to the promptings of the Holy spirit or have you allowed distractions to come in the way? What steps can you take to align your actions with the simple directions the Holy Spirit is giving you?*

- *How are you currently caring for your body? Do you know that to do God's work on earth, we need to care for our bodies? Are you consistent in exercising regularly to maintain physical fitness? Do you stay hydrated by drinking adequate amount of water each day? Are you mindful of dietary choices, opting for nutritious foods that nourish your body? Have you scheduled an annual check? If not, write down the barriers and obstacles preventing you from this, and what steps you can take to prioritize well-being moving forward.*

CHAPTER SIX

ALL TRUTH

"Nevertheless, I tell you the truth. It is to your advantage that I go away; for if I do not go away, the helper will not come to you; but if I depart, I will send him to you. And when he has come, he will convict the world of sin, and of righteousness, and judgment of sin, because they do not believe in Me; Of righteousness, because I go to My Father and you see me no more; Of judgment, because the ruler of this world is judged. I still have many things to say to you, but you cannot bear them now. However, when he, the spirit of truth, has come, he will guide you into all truth; for he will not speak on his authority, but whatever he hears, he will speak, and he will tell you of things to come."
John 16:7-13 (NKJV).

After watching Dr. Creflo Dollar's message 'manifesting healing' on Youtube, I wrote down all the steps he highlighted in my journal. The Holy Spirit, who is our helper, guided me to understand this truth in a way unique to my journey. He described them as 'weapons'. You can also call them 'keys'.

> *"For the weapons of our warfare are not carnal*
> *but mighty in God for pulling down strongholds."*
> *2 Corinthians 10:4 (NKJV).*

In the kingdom of God, we have our modus operandi, which means the way things are done. It's called our rules of engagement. The bible teaches that when Jesus died and was resurrected, he left believers with many gifts and promises, foremost of which is the Holy Spirit. He is considered our advantage. The journey and fight of our faith is not one we can navigate by ourselves. That's why God said we need the Holy Spirit, our divine helper and encourager, who will guide us into all truth. He will help us navigate seasons and difficult situations. "What are these weapons?" you may ask. They are steps we take to enforce our victory. As believers, we need to know these keys so that we know what to do in the time of adversity. We use these weapons to enforce our victory with the help of the Holy Spirit.

I cracked the code for my unique journey by leveraging the Holy Spirit to guide me into ***all truth***. For one, this can look like him asking you to use one of these weapons. For another, it could be an instruction to use all, or it could be none, as He might give new instructions together. The key is to lean on him for your specific journey.

COMMUNION

"For I received from the lord that which I also delivered to you; that the Lord Jesus on the same night in which he was betrayed took bread, and when he had given thanks, he broke it and said, "Take, eat; this is my body which is broken for you; do this in remembrance of me. In this same manner, he also took the cup after supper saying, "This cup of the new covenant in my blood, This do as often as you drink it, in remembrance of me."
1 Corinthians 11:23-25 (NKJV).

The act of taking communion, which is also called breaking bread was done at the last supper before Jesus' death. Jesus asked that we do this in remembrance of him. I leveraged this advantage given to us as believers a whole lot, and I still do. It is an act of obedience. A good practice is to declare the word of God while taking it. I usually say, "This is your body broken for me and as I eat it I remember the finished works of Jesus, the blood of Jesus speaks better things concerning me than the blood of Abel." Taking communion is not only a weapon but a sure step towards victory. This is a weapon or a key that God has given us. The blood of Jesus has a voice, and it speaks mercy and better things than the blood of Abel.

"To Jesus the mediator of the new covenant, and to the blood of sprinkling that speaks better things than that of Abel."
Hebrews 12:24 (NKJV).

Dr. Creflo Dollar said, "I took communion like a prescription every day. The communion elements can be anything; It doesn't matter what you use to symbolize it. Some communion wafers and wine sets are sold, but even when those were not available, I used crackers, juice, and water. I took it every day. What matters is the faith you have and what it represents. I would feel alive, rejuvenated, whole. The power of God showed up," he said.

Communion is very powerful and makes a huge difference. By taking the blood, we are remembering the finished works of Jesus-that by his stripes, we were healed. I mean already healed, not trying to be healed - a done deal. The blood of Jesus is a powerful weapon; it avenges, it speaks mercy over judgment, and it is not just a symbol-it is life. I also used anything available as a representation when I did not have the communion elements. What matters is what it stands for, not about the elements used, but understanding what it is represents-taking the life of Jesus and exchanging our weakness for God's wholeness. Taking it regularly is an act of obedience.

"For the life of the flesh is in the blood, and I have given it to you upon the altar to make atonement for your souls; for it is the blood that makes atonement for the soul.
Leviticus 17:11 (NKJV)

Principles

1. *Taking the body and the blood regularly, as often as you can, is taking life and enforcing victory.*
2. *The blood of Jesus is life and has a voice that speaks mercy.*
3. *Taking communion is an act of obedience.*
4. *Elements are not limited to bread and wine, crackers, and water; anything similar works too.*

5. *Your heart and your faith matter when taking communion obediently.*

Self-introspection Questions.   •

*   *What do you know about the significance of the blood of Jesus to the body of Christ and to your life?*
*   *What intentional steps are you taking to leverage the significance of communion and allowing it to inspire greater devotion and commitment in your walk with God?*

THE WORD OF GOD

**"For assuredly, I say to you, whoever says
to this mountain, be removed and be cast
into the sea, and does not doubt in his heart
but believes that those things he says will be
done, he will have whatever he says."
Mark 11:23 (NKJV)**

We shall have what we say, it's a given in the kingdom of God. Confessing the word is a very important weapon and key to our Christian faith. One thing I did was at every point in my journey was to make sure I had a word from God, which I confessed and declared as often as I could. Throughout the journey, I made declarations from the word of God such as "I will not die but live to declare the goodness of God in the land of the living," "I dwell in the secret place of the lord under the shadow of the Almighty," "He will not allow the sickness to kill me," "With long life shall he satisfy me," "I speak to the mountains be thou removed," "My body responds to treatment," "My cells are rejuvenated," "I am healthy," "The blood of Jesus speaks for me," "Ten thousand may fall by my left and right hand side it will not come near me." I declared what I wanted to see.

There were times I had negative thoughts crop up such as, "Can't you see people dying from cancer every day? Do you realize they are people better than you, more righteous than you? They've done more things for God and they are more connected to fathers of faith. Look at tiny you- how will you make it?" I had only the word of God as a weapon. I would respond by saying, "My case is different. The Bible says, "A thousand may fall by my side, ten thousand at my right-hand side, I shall only behold it with my eyes, but it will not come near me." I had to keep making these confessions intentionally for all I wanted to see. I was constantly enforcing and declaring the word of God as often as I could. Our words are life, and the enemy usually comes subtly into our minds through thoughts and suggestions. They become words and deeds if we don't watch them. We need to take authority over our thoughts always, casting down imaginations and bringing every thought to the obedience of Christ this is by speaking the word of God. A lot of times, even when declaring the word of God, it may seem like nothing is happening, but a lot is happening. The words we speak are spirit and life.

"It is the spirit who gives life; the flesh profits nothing. The words that I speak to you are spirit, and they are life."
John 6:63 (NKJV)

Sometimes, the symptoms may even get worse, and other times we might get a worse report from the doctor. The truth is something is still happening. Keep believing and don't let the enemy lie to you. It is important to keep declaring the word. The word of God is potent, and it always works. Power lies not just in having the word but in confessing it. God formed the world with words, and the word is our authority. This principle still holds. I learned to declare in the past tense like it had already happened: "My scan was all clear and I was declared free from this diagnosis." As believers, whenever negative thoughts come, we use the weapon of God's word in warfare. You must intentionally speak the word.

"Let the redeemed of the lord SAY so, whom he has redeemed from the hand of the enemy." Psalm 107:2 (NKJV).

Principles

1. *We have a singular responsibility in the face of a challenge which is to speak the word to it.*
2. *In the kingdom of God, we shall have what we say.*
3. *We need to know the word of God so that we can declare it at any negative thought, no matter the results we see.*
4. *It is our obligation to search out the word of God, and spend time reading it daily, even before a challenging season comes up, leveraging the help of the Holy Spirit.*
5. *We have to speak the word, not just think it or know it; we are speaking spirits.*

Self-introspection Questions

- *Write in your journal the word of God you are currently holding onto for any challenging situation. Take out sometime to meditate and declare these scriptures to allow their truth to penetrate your heart.*

- *Write down ways you can challenge and resist negative thoughts. Pen down positive affirmations and truth that you will use to bring negative and defeating thoughts into captivity and obedience.*

FAITH IS VICTORY

"Now Faith is the substance of things hoped for, the evidence of things not seen."
Hebrews11:1 (NKJV).

Faith is a positive response to the finished works of Jesus. One of my spiritual fathers, Pastor Poju Oyemade of Covenant nation, puts it as "faith is the believer's voice of victory." We must have faith, even if it is as small as a mustard seed. We must release our faith for healing and anything we believe God for. In the kingdom of God, faith is a currency we spend. We must believe whatever God says is ours in his word by faith.

"Now, a certain woman had a flow of blood for twelve years. And had suffered many things from many physicians. She had spent all that she had and was no better, but rather grew worse. When she heard about Jesus, she came behind him in the crowd and touched his garment. For she said, "If only I may touch his clothes, I shall be made well. "Immediately the fountain of her blood was dried up, and she felt in her body that she was healed of the affliction. And Jesus, immediately knowing in himself

*that power had gone out of him, turned around in
the crowd and said, "Who touched my clothes?"
But his disciples said to him, "You see the multitude
thronging you, and you say "Who touched me?"
And he looked around to see her who had done
this thing. But the woman, fearing and trembling,
knowing what had happened to her, came and fell
down before him and told him the whole truth. And
he said to her, "Daughter, your faith has made you
well. Go in peace, and be healed of your affliction."*
Mark 5:25-33 (NKJV).

The woman with the issue of blood made a connection with her faith to get healed. There were so many people around Jesus, but she was different because her faith drew virtue from Jesus. And he asked, "Who touched me?" God responds to our faith, that's our part of the deal. The woman knew what she wanted; she was brutally focused, and Jesus responded to her faith. It was her faith that made her distinct in the crowd. Her faith connected her with Jesus, and virtue was released. Like that woman, we must dare to believe.

*"For whatever is born of God overcomes
the world. And this is the victory that has
overcome the world -our faith."*
1 John 5:4 (NKJV).

Faith is a currency that we spend. We cannot afford to be devoid of faith, even if it is as little as a mustard seed. Faith is a spiritual force, so natural reasoning will not pull any triggers. Faith is the trigger we need to pull.

*"But without faith, it is impossible to please
him, for he who comes to God must believe
that he is, and that he is a rewarder of
those who diligently seek him."*
Hebrews 11:6 (NKJV).

It's also important to know how faith comes. Faith comes by hearing and hearing the word of God. We need to fill our hearts with the knowledge of the word of God. That way, we carry weight in the spirit, and we are not featherweight Christians that faint in the face of adversity.

*"So then faith comes by hearing and
hearing by the word of God."*
Romans 10:17 (NKJV).

Principles

1. *We must release our faith, even if it's as small as a mustard seed.*
2. *Faith is the believer's voice of victory.*
3. *God responds to our faith; it is a prerequisite for victory in the kingdom of God.*
4. *Faith is a currency we spend in the kingdom.*
5. *Our faith is increased by the knowledge of God's word; we need to fill our hearts with the word of God.*

Self-introspection Questions

- *Journal about the challenging areas of your life in which you need to activate your faith. What intentional steps can you take by faith to enable you draw strength from God in these challenging situations?*

- *What deliberate steps can you take to cultivate a deeper sense of trust and reliance on God's provision and grace? What actions are you taking to invest in the knowledge of God's word daily?*

SEED

"And he moved from there to the mountain east of Bethel, and he pitched his tent with Bethel on the west and Ai on the east, there he built an altar to the lord and called on the name of the Lord."
Genesis 12:8 (NKJV)

There was a season when the Holy Spirit gave me an instruction to listen to some specific messages on Youtube by a woman of God whom I greatly admire, Architect Olajumoke Adenowo. She spoke about altars. I learned that raising an altar sometimes involves giving an offering that costs me something-in other words, something sacrificial. This act can in turn open a portal, an access point.

"Then King David said to Ornan, "No, but I will surely buy it for the full price, for I will not take what is yours for the Lord, nor offer burnt offerings with that which costs me nothing."
1 Chronicles 21:24(NKJV).

"To open a portal or to receive a higher dimension of warfare. Something may need to leave your hand," she explained. The Holy Spirit helped me understand that an altar can sometimes be represented by a seed. It could be a financial substance, a sacrifice of praise, worship, or many other things. In my case, I was instructed by the Holy Spirit to raise an altar to God in the form of a sacrificial financial seed. I knew the battle was bigger than me, and I needed to engage a higher dimension of warfare. By following this instruction, I aligned myself with Gods will and created a point of contact for his blessings.

Again, this is not a one-size-fits-all, but the crux is that the Holy Spirit will guide you into *all truth*, which may look different for everyone. I was led to sow these financial seeds into the life of a ministry. This was him guiding me into the truth unique to my journey. It is important to walk with God so that he can open up the unique code for your situation; you need to crack the code. For one it could be a seed; for another, a deed; It could also be something else entirely. The key is to follow the Holy Spirit's guidance by having our radar fine-tuned to him all the time. Giving a financial seed is not a rigid principle. In my case, it was a weapon. An instruction was given to me, and I did it in obedience.

Principles

1. *You may be led to take a specific step that would represent raising an altar.*
2. *It's important to listen to specific instructions by the holy spirit, to be sensitive to his prompts, and to crack the code.*
3. *Instructions can look different for everyone; lean into God for yours.*
4. *Seeds are weapons in the kingdom; they open portals.*
5. *Whatever the instruction looks like, it's important to obey.*

Self-introspection Questions

- *Have you received any specific instructions or promptings from the Holy Spirit? What steps in obedience are you taking in response to these instructions?*
- *Write a prayer asking God for clarity, discernment, and grace to follow through with regards to the unique instructions he gives you.*

MERCY

> **"Let us therefore come boldly to the throne
> of grace, that we may obtain mercy and
> find grace to help in the time of need."**
> **Hebrews 4:16 (NKJV).**

God's mercy triumphs over judgment. I was so ill, so weak I could hardly walk or eat. I couldn't even pray. I just had to latch onto God's mercy. A lot of times, I said one single line of prayer: 'Lord, have mercy.' I knew that it was only by his grace and mercy that I would not be consumed. This was challenging. This season led me to know that it's not about works; it's about God's mercy. God's Mercy is available to all his children and his mercies are new every morning.

> **"Surely Goodness and mercy shall follow
> me, all the days of my life; and I will dwell
> in the house of the Lord forever."**
> **Psalm 23:6 (NKJV).**

I held onto the scripture that says his steadfast love never ceases and his mercies never come to an end. God's mercy, not our efforts, is the key. It's important to be a daily recipient of his mercy. Whatever you are facing, tap into his mercy; they are new every morning.

"Through the lord's mercies, we are not consumed, because his compassions fail not. They are new every morning; great is your faithfulness."
Lamentations 3:22-23 (NKJV).

Principles

1. *God's mercy triumphs over judgment.*
2. *When going through a tough time, it's pivotal to latch onto God's mercy every day.*
3. *There is a fresh supply of new mercy every morning for God's children.*
4. *It is by his mercy we are not consumed.*
5. *God's mercy is available to all; we need to come boldly to the throne to obtain it.*

Self-introspection Questions

- *How often do you pray to God for mercy? Do you set aside dedicated time each day to commune with God in prayer, thereby latching onto his mercies, or do you allow busyness and distractions to hinder your prayer life?*
- *What steps can you take to learn more about Gods mercy? What books can you read? What scriptures can you engage to cultivate a deeper and more vibrant connection with God mercy?*

LET LOVE LEAD

God loves you and me. He is intentional about his children. When we go through hard seasons, it's important to understand that he is not angry with us. When we understand this and embrace our Christian walk from this vantage point, we will realize the power of embracing God's love. He gave his only son to die for us. When he sees us, he sees his son, the righteousness of God. When you keep this in view, it becomes a source of grace, allowing you to extend love to yourself and others. Love is a weapon. One day, the Holy Spirit said to me, "Let love lead."

"Search me, O God, and know my heart, try me and know my anxieties, And see if there is any wicked way in me. And lead me in the way everlasting."
Psalm 139:23-24 (NKJV).

I knew my healing journey meant I needed to choose love over offense, bitterness, and unforgiveness. That way, my heart will be light. I embraced love as a weapon. Love is a force; It enables us to rise above past hurts, releasing all the negativity that burdens our hearts. Sometimes, it may be past wounds, rejection, depression, and suppressed emotions. That is why the Holy Spirit is our helper and he guides us into *all truth*. He will shed light on every dark and hidden matter of the heart, and he will reveal blind spots. I chose *love*, I *let love lead*, I embraced God's love. This became a force enabling me to look past hurts, bitterness, and unforgiveness, lifting me above inflicted pain encountered on my life's journey. In turn, it helped me extend love to others.

Whatever your journey may look like, ***let love lead***. Regardless of your past and gruesome encounters in any phase and stage of life, it's vital to release the burdens, allowing love to navigate the difficult parts of your journey and free both you and others.

> **"Beloved, let us love one another, for**
> **love is of God; and everyone who loves**
> **is born of God and knows God."**
> **1 John 4:7 (NKJV)**

Principles

1. *Engage the weapon of love;Let love lead.*
2. *Allow God to help you heal from past hurts, offenses, rejection, issues of your past.*
3. *God loves you, let this be your vantage point as you go through challenging times.*
4. *Loving other people is evidence that you know God.*
5. *Strive to walk in love and forgiveness by the help of the Holy Spirit.*

Self-introspection Questions

- *Write down scriptures or promises in God's word that remind you of God's unfailing love and grace towards you. Do you allow yourself to fully receive and embrace God's love, or do you struggle with feelings of unworthiness and inadequacy?*
- *Journal about any hurts that you may have found hard to let go of. Write down steps you can take to **let love lead** above all offenses, pain, and past guilt in every area of your life. Are you intentional about meditating on truths and allowing them to shape your perspective on life?*

PRAISE IS A WEAPON

Praise is a weapon. I describe it as a *master* key, no matter what the situation looks like. It is a weapon that I have wielded in the darkest times. A story comes to mind one of my close friends faced an unimaginable ordeal. She was pregnant with twins, and when she was about six months gone, one of the twins died in utero (in her belly). The only thing the doctors could do was to keep the dead twin in there while the twin that was alive grew. This was the best way to save the life of the living baby. It was a high-risk situation. Thankfully, she gave birth to a live twin, and the dead fetus was removed. But then, as you can imagine, she developed life-threatening complications which landed her in ICU (Intensive care unit) immediately after childbirth. The doctors tried their best to stabilize her vital signs to no avail. One morning, a doctor came into her room and said, "We've done all we can. Nothing is working. We are not able to control anything. If you are a Christian pray." That night, she resolved in her heart to do something different as she had been praying all along. She rose from her bed and had a serious intentional session of praise to the father, she danced and danced despite it all, she declared her gratitude. By the next morning, she had turned a corner 100%. Everything changed 100%. Her blood pressure became normal, and all her vitals were stable. The situation had transformed.

> "But at midnight, Paul and Silas were praying and singing hymns to God, and the prisoners were listening to them. Suddenly, there was a great earthquake, so that the foundations of the prison were shaken, and immediately all doors were opened, and everyone's chains were loosed."
> Acts 16:25-26 (NKJV).

I've learned to praise God and rejoice through difficult seasons, recognizing that he holds the blueprint of my life. He is always in charge, so I give him praise regardless of what the report is. It's no longer a case of my cup being half full or half empty. For me, more importantly, I have a cup. When you operate from this vantage point, it doesn't matter how bad the situation is; you will see a silver lining, a reason to be grateful in that dark cloud. I choose to remain thankful always. A thankful heart finds reasons to be grateful.

> *"Though the fig tree may not blossom, nor fruit be on the vines, though the labor of the olive may fail. And the fields yield no food; Though the flock may be cut off from the fold, and there be no herd in the stalls. Yet I will rejoice in the lord; I will joy in the God of my salvation!" Habakkuk 3:17-18 (NKJV).*

Principles

1. *Praise is a key, an infallible weapon in the kingdom.*
2. *Praise confuses the enemy.*
3. *Praise turns things around; you may not feel like it, that's what makes it a sacrifice of praise.*
4. *God inhabits our praises, and he moves when we give a sacrifice of praise.*
5. *Regardless of what is happening on the outside, don't let that deter you, praise God, and dance to him intentionally through the difficult seasons.*

Self-introspection Questions

- *Write down intentional steps you can take to activate praise mode in your life. Do you recognize the importance of praise and worship and having a heart of gratitude no matter the circumstance?*
- *It's important to cultivate a lifestyle of joy and praise. Do you have a worship playlist you listen to when you are in high or low spirits?*

THE NAME OF JESUS

"The name of the lord is a strong tower; the righteous run to it, and they are safe."
Proverbs 18:10 (NKJV).

One thing I noticed was the moment I was diagnosed and knew the name of what was wrong with me, the fear of the unknown ceased. This is because there is a *name* that is *above every other name*. There is a name above "*cancer*". There is a name that every knee must bow to; the name of **JESUS.** The name of Jesus is a weapon; that's why we pray and declare the name. It doesn't matter what the name of the disease or the mountain or challenge is, what matters is the name that is above all names. We have a name that is above every name, the name at which every knee must bow to. I kept declaring the word of God over my life in the name of Jesus.

"Therefore God also has highly exalted him and given him the name which is above every name that at the name of Jesus, every knee should bow of those in heaven and of those on earth and

of those under the earth and that every tongue should confess that Jesus Christ is lord to the glory of God and every tongue confesses that Jesus is lord., to the glory of God the father."
Philippians 2:9-11 (NKJV).

Principles

1. *There is a name above every name; the name of JESUS.*
2. *So long as your situation has a name be assured that there is a greater name.*
3. *Pray in the name of Jesus over that situation; it is a weapon.*
4. *The name of the lord is a safe space.*
5. *Every situation and diagnosis will bow to the name of Jesus.*

Self-introspection Questions.

- *In your journal, write down the names of God that resonate with you deeply, the names of jesus that you have experienced personally, such as Jehovah Rapha, my healer. Do you use these names in prayer and devotion to God?*
- *What name do you call upon first when you face a challenge? Do you call on friends, family, or the name of the lord? Do you know the importance of praying in the name of Jesus?*

In our unique journeys, the holy spirit will guide us into **ALL TRUTH**. This can look like exactly what to do, what steps to take, and of course, many more keys that are not listed here. The most important thing is to leverage this advantage we have, which is *the Holy Spirit,* by spending time with and obeying him. That way, he will guide us into all truth and ensure that the victory is ours.

CHAPTER SEVEN

THE GIFT OF MEN

I had an interesting encounter the week I got discharged from the hospital. I was scheduled for an appointment with Dr. Smith in his office. I booked an Uber (a ride-hailing service). The driver arrived, and I got into the car. I had not spoken to anyone about what was going on except my husband, who was out of town. I wasn't ready to talk about it yet; it was fresh. This was only two days after I got discharged.

"Hello," he said in a Spanish accent. "Good morning," I replied. I was not in a chatty mood. After a few minutes into the ride, "Do you mind if I ask you a question? Is there something in your body?" he asked. "What do you mean?" I replied, quite shocked and unsure what he meant. "I'm good," I added. The question was unusual and caught me unawares because I generally do not talk when I am taking an Uber ride. "No, ma'am, I mean, is there something around your stomach region?" he insisted. "Hmm, actually, yes," I muttered, very surprised. "I just got diagnosed. There's a mass in that region, and I am on my way to a doctor's appointment." "God told me this morning that I would pick someone up with something around there. He asked me to tell you. He is with you. His name will be glorified," he added. I felt the presence of God so strong that I burst out wailing. This was a stranger, yet I felt overwhelmed by emotions, and he began to pray and worship. The reassuring power of the love of God wrapped me up. I felt God's presence so strongly in that ride. He started praying in the Spirit, playing worship music, and we just started to worship. That car ride was like a Holy Ghost service; the power of God was so strong. He dropped me off and encouraged me with God's word. I was short of words. God sent a stranger to comfort me as I knew I was all alone. Who am I, Lord, that you are mindful of me?

> **"What is man, that you are mindful of him,**
> **And the son of man that you visit him?"**
> **Psalm 8:4 (NKJV).**

I got a call from a lady from my insurance company. She introduced herself as a care navigator. The insurance company had informed her about the recent diagnosis. This was after my discharge and was the usual insurance protocol. She was my invisible friend, a compassionate voice on the other end of the line in the early part of my journey. She became my confidante, and her weekly calls became a lifeline. Before I started treatment, she asked about the next steps, how I felt, the emotions I was experiencing, the scans, test results, and the doctor's plan. I looked forward to these conversations with her. She was my secret friend, guiding me through the journey that takes an undeniable toll. This turned out to be a great psychological support. At that point, I hadn't opened up to anybody other than my husband, and she became a great source of strength. She guided me, answering questions about what to expect from treatment and offering a voice of reason. In retrospect, she was truly pivotal in my journey, taking me from a place of silence to vocalizing my thoughts aiding my mental health.

Another experience that marked my journey was one time when I got admitted to the hospital due to complications from chemotherapy. It was New Year's Day, and I was really sad and tired. A doctor walked into my room and introduced herself as a Nigerian, like I am. She had seen my name on the medical records as one of her patients that night; she was the internist on call, and she felt the need to come up to say hello to me. Wow, I was touched. This was such a lonely season for me. I was pretty much on my own as I intentionally did not let people in, as I explained earlier. As she spoke with me, I felt an overwhelming sense of connection. Her presence brought comfort and warmth. She encouraged me and prayed for me. Being a Christian, she reminded me to believe the report of the Lord. I got emotional and burst into tears. She encouraged me with God's word and prayed with me. Those words, coming from a stranger felt like a divine message. Later, she brought me a card that had the scripture:

*"But those who wait on the lord shall renew
their strength; they shall mount up with
wings like eagles, they shall run and not be
weary, they shall walk and not faint."
Isiah 40:31 (NKJV).*

God had sent another stranger to ease my journey. The kind words of affirmation lifted my spirit when I needed it the most. I once heard someone say that she receives her friends from God. This challenged what I previously believed. While it's good to choose friends, it's awesome to receive friends from God. Trust me, this revelation struck a chord with me, highlighting that there is a level where God selects people for our unique and individual journeys. For some, it's friends; for others, it's the blessing of an amazing, close-knit family. Some are lucky to have both. No matter what it looks like for you, the important thing is to know that God can be trusted to give you the right people to support your journey.

> *"A friend loves at all times, and a*
> *brother is born for adversity."*
> *Proverbs 17:17 (NKJV).*

My journey emphasized the importance of God-given relationships and revealed that people are God's gifts, diverse and unexpected. Apostle Joshua Selman teaches a lot about relationships. In one of his messages, he taught that 'God blesses men, through men to men'. This lesson reshaped my perspective, teaching me to honor all men and view them as vessels of God. It challenged me to be intentionally supportive and empathic, going beyond surface level to becoming the friend who steps in without being asked, ready to ease people's journeys.

> *"Honor all people. Love the brotherhood.*
> *Fear god. Honor the king."*
> *1 Peter 2:17 (NKJV).*

God can be trusted for good friendships. I have been a part of a prayer group called 'Woman of Destiny' for over 20 years. From my university days until now, we have prayed together almost every

Saturday over the years via our online platform. The irony of this group is that we all bumped into one another coincidentally, but now in hindsight, God connected us. This tribe demonstrates how God consistently places people in our journeys to provide support and aid our destiny. Throughout my health journey, these ladies carried me even without knowing the details of what was going on with me. They were a constant presence, offering prayers and most notably carrying me towards the end as I faced surgery. They initiated a prayer chain that lasted nearly a week, covering every aspect of the process. Despite the complexity of the surgery, everything went smoothly. I am forever grateful for a godly support system. It is such a privilege. God can indeed be trusted to connect you with the right people. It can be a church community for some, or just a prayer partner for another. Ultimately, it's important to be led by the Holy Spirit.

"For as many as are led by the spirit of God, these are the sons of God."
Romans 8:14 (NKJV).

Contrary to the world's narrative, God can be trusted for a good marriage- a partner who will go through thick and thin, for better or for worse, with you. They say who you marry matters, and I can testify to this. A gift that keeps on giving is my husband. He is such a rock, and everything he represents and how he eased my journey leaves me without a doubt that he is nothing but a gift from God.

I had moved into my sister- in- law's house after I started to feel better. I was there for over a year. Her home was a launch pad for getting oriented to life again. This was such a critical phase in recovery for me and the kids. Her support was immense. Having an amazing family to support us as we regained stability was divinely orchestrated by God. I am forever grateful for the gift of amazing and selfless people.

**"The king's heart is in the hand of the lord, like the rivers of water; he turns it wherever he wishes."
Proverbs 21:1 (NKJV).**

I had reconnected with one of my long-time friends within that season. At the onset, she was the one I always complained to about the funny symptoms I was noticing in my body. I was scared to go to the hospital. One day, she called me and was so firm in her words. "You must go into the hospital! You need to know the root cause of this weakness you have been complaining about," she said. Her words resonated so loud, reiterating what my husband had been saying. At that point, I knew I had no choice; I had to go in, which led to the initial visit to Dr. Kelly. After the diagnosis, she never probed about the details, even though I later realized she had an idea. This helped me a great deal because she would call, and we would talk at length about every other thing but never about the diagnosis. She never brought it up. This really helped me to deflect, which aided my mental health. She was so instrumental in my journey; she was God-sent.

I share an incredible story of another friend of mine. We hadn't spoken in three years since the start of the pandemic, and truth be told, I had lost touch with most people. She recounted that she had just walked out of a store, when, out of the blue, my name dropped in her heart. She searched for my number, which she didn't have anymore. Then she remembered she had my resume, and my number was on it. Not sure it was still the same, she decided to give me a call. To her surprise, I picked it up. It was a pleasant surprise for me as well since I had been incommunicado for three years, withdrawn for the most part as my coping mechanism. I found it amazing that she would call. We chatted, and upon hearing about what had happened and that I was already in recovery, she flew into my state of residence, which was hours away from hers. She treated me to a great time and ensured I and my kids had fun. Financially, she supported me without asking, understanding I hadn't been able to work in three years. Before each follow-up doctor appointment, she would brainstorm with me on the questions to ask. She practically attended doctor visits with me virtually. She was there for me. After surgery, I was given a special restricted diet. I was too tired to pay attention, which led to eating the wrong food and resulted in readmission. She went above and beyond. She took all the doctors' instructions and recommendations, read them, sat me down, and meticulously guided me on what to eat and what to avoid, especially considering the temporary ileostomy bag I had post-surgery. She did all this while cheering me on and encouraging me that we were at the end of the journey. Her support was beyond what I could have imagined or asked for. This marked my heart as it was clearly another example of receiving a friend from God. This experience revealed the truth of scripture:

"A man who has friends must himself be friendly, But there is a friend who sticks closer than a brother."
Proverbs 18:24 (NKJV).

This showed me that God is indeed in the business of placing the right people with the right capacity in our lives in the right season. He is our ultimate source.

On the flip side, interestingly, God can choose to take some people out of our lives, sometimes against our will. It can be for a season, or for a reason, but it's important to trust that God sees and knows what we do not. A very important lesson the Holy Spirit taught me in that season was that not everyone will have the capacity to be there for you like others in trying times, which is okay. Support can look different in different seasons and come from different people. Not everyone can play the same role, and it's crucial to give them grace and understand that everyone has their own hard journey that you may not even be aware of.

Sometimes, when people in our family or friends do not come through for us the way we envision, we may feel disappointed, neglected, and betrayed. This is normal, but it is important to preserve our joy, which is the best way to stay above offense and bitterness. I once heard someone say that those who are meant to be in that scene of the movie of your life would show up, those who are not meant to be will not. Some may feature fully at the beginning, some in the middle, but they may not have the capacity to be there till the end. Whichever way it plays out, it's still okay. We should be thankful for them regardless. God is the ultimate scriptwriter. No matter what the journey looks like, we keep our focus on him. Not on man, not on people.

> *"Do not put your trust in princes, nor in the*
> *son of man, in whom there is no help."*
> *Psalm 146:3 (NKJV).*

Keeping this in perspective will enable us to journey through life without carrying unnecessary baggage of offense, bitterness, and unforgiveness. Knowing that the only one that has the capacity and bandwidth to always be with us in this journey of life is the *one* who is guaranteed to never leave us or forsake us;-the Holy Spirit.

"For he himself has said, "I will never leave you nor forsake you." Hebrews 13:5b(NKJV).

Also, it's good to keep in mind that in a time or season when a friend, family member, or colleague goes silent, instead of making assumptions, we should consider lifting them up in prayer. When that name drops in your heart, take a moment to pray and maybe check in on them if you can. Most importantly, be led by the Holy Spirit. Even if they are not forthcoming, remember everyone has their silent challenges that often go unnoticed. Let us pray for our friends genuinely and aim to be better friends as well. Because when life gets dark and daunting, we need one another.

"And the lord restored job losses when he prayed for his friends. Indeed, the lord gave Job twice as much as he had before." Job 42:10 (NKJV).

Undeniably, God blessed me with the gift of men in multifaceted ways - physically, spiritually, emotionally, and mentally -all provided by the various individuals that God intentionally placed in my life. A robust support system for navigating difficult times, such as a health crisis, can only be from God. He orchestrated a beautiful symphony to ease my journey.

Principles

1. *God's blessing comes to men through fellow men.*
2. *It's imperative to honor all people.*
3. *It's good to choose friends but then, it's great to receive friends from God.*
4. *Guard your heart, and move away from offense and disappointment by the help of the Holy Spirit.*
5. *Keep your eyes always focused on the one who promised he would never leave or forsake you.*
6. *Get plugged into a church, or fellowship, having a community is rewarding.*
7. *God is mindful of you.*
8. *Strive to be the type of friend that sticks closer than a brother.*
9. *Pray for your friends.*
10. *Don't do life alone.*

Self-introspection Questions.

- *Write down the names of the individuals in your life whom you believe are gifts from God. What steps have you taken to acknowledge and appreciate them for their unique qualities and contributions and how they enrich your life?*
- *Do you use your time, resources, and talents to bless and support your friends? Do you take time to pray for your friends? If not, make a resolve today to pray for your friends more often.*
- *Think about those friends you have not heard from in a while. Write down their names, and with the help of the Holy Spirit, consider reaching out to them, a word of encouragement could go a long way.*

CHAPTER EIGHT

SUPERNATURAL VERSUS SPECTACULAR

I had responded well to immunotherapy treatment and started to gain weight. Symptoms reversed, bleeding stopped, and tumor markers and numbers returned to normal. No evidence of cancer was detected in my blood. The realization hit me- this was *supernatural healing*. I had come from a place where chemotherapy did not work, making the success of immunotherapy even more profound.

On one of my hospital visits, Dr. Bally said, "We made a good move! And because of your case, we have now witnessed changes in treatment protocol." he added. "More people are getting healed because we are putting this new line of treatment forward. We are now treating people with immunotherapy as a second line of treatment." he explained. This was amazing to hear. My journey had opened new doors for others walking similar paths.

*"Which none of the rulers of this age
knew; for had they known, they would
not have crucified the lord of glory."*
1 Corinthians 2:8 (NKJV)

I read a story of a man on social media who was ill and found out he had elevated tumor markers signaling cancer. He joined a popular online prayer altar and was miraculously healed, with the markers returning to normal without going through any treatment. *This was spectacular.* This was an amazing testament to God's power. This testimony was etched on my soul. I also desired such a spectacular move of God. This was around the time that Dr. Bally explained that oftentimes immunotherapy could work so well in some people that the tumor would disappear and there would be no need for surgery. I started to pray that the scan scheduled for post-treatment would show such a spectacular result of instant, total healing. As I got scheduled for another MRI, I prayed, and had faith that the result would eliminate the need for surgery. I prayed, declared, and had faith. I eagerly awaited MRI results, hoping to be among the few immunotherapy success stories. I craved a spectacular intervention.

*"Then he said, "Go out and stand on the mountain
before the lord." And behold, the lord passed by,
and a great and strong wind tore into the mountains
and broke the rocks in pieces before the lord, but
the lord was not in the wind, and after the wind, an
earthquake, but the lord was not in the earthquake,
and after the earthquake a fire, but the lord was
not in the fire; and after the fire a still small voice.
So, it was then Elijah heard it, that he wrapped his
face in his mantle and went out and stood in the*

entrance of the cave. Suddenly a voice came to him, and said, "What are you doing here, Elijah?" 1 Kings 19:11-13(NKJV).

One of my spiritual fathers, Pastor Poju Oyemade once taught about the *supernatural versus. the spectacular.* He explained the above scripture, saying Elijah expected God to move through the wind, earthquake, and fire, but the lord came as the sound of a gentle blowing wind. "Oftentimes, we look out for the spectacular, not realizing that the supernatural is present every time." he said. The truth is that God works in mysterious ways, choosing to do things through any means he so desires. It can be supernatural or spectacular; the choice is his, all to the glory of his name.

A couple of days after the MRI, I got a call from Dr. Bally. "The MRI report is out," he said. "Okay," I replied eagerly. "The good news is the tumor shrunk significantly, and it's like a bag of popcorn as tumor markers are normal. But we still need to get it out," he explained. "I'm afraid we've passed the threshold for immunotherapy; further treatment will not do much anymore. I would want Dr. Smith to schedule you for surgery," he added. "Wow," I said, as a wave of disappointment passed over me from hearing something other than what I expected. "Thank you, Dr. Bally," I managed to mutter as I dropped the phone. I was a bit down because I did not want surgery, but I didn't let the disappointment linger. I remembered Pastor Poju had taught us that what we do in the first minute of a crisis matters and that our initial response is crucial. I started pacing my room, saying, "Lord, I will yet praise You. Even though this was not the news I was expecting, I will yet praise you." I praised him intentionally, repeating, "I will yet praise You. I surrender to God's perfect plan," even though I wanted it another way. Then suddenly, I saw the light in the situation, and I had a new perspective. At least there was now an option for surgery, which was still *supernatural*. I was finally at the point where surgery was now an option. Thankfully, initially, it wasn't an option as the tumor was too large, but here I am with a way out. The treatment had worked, and this in itself is supernatural.

A lot of times, the difference lies in our perspective. We desire the spectacular, which makes us lose focus on the fact that the supernatural is happening every day in many ways. This desire for the spectacular causes us to miss the everyday miracles and the sure mercies that surround us.

"Incline your ear and come to me. Hear, and your soul shall live; And I will make an everlasting covenant with you – The sure mercies of David."
Isiah 55:3 (NKJV).

Surgery became the next action plan; it was inevitable at this point. It was going to be a four-hour procedure to remove what was left of the tumor. As the surgery day drew closer, I started to feel uneasy and a bit nervous. Being a doctor doesn't help sometimes because we know too much. My mind began to bug me, and it seemed like I started to consider the storm around me. I felt like I was walking on water, and when I started to consider the storm, I began to sink.

I shared my feelings with Ladipo, my younger brother, and what he said marked my heart. He reassured me, saying "Sometimes God wants us to go through the process despite our desire for shortcuts. Even Jesus did not want to go to the cross," he added. That was profound and gave me the perspective I needed to face the upcoming surgery.

"O My father, if it is possible, let this cup pass from me nevertheless, not as I will, but as you will."
Matthew 26:39 (NKJV)

As the week leading up to surgery came, the Holy Spirit gave me an instruction- *recenter*. I had to deliberately and intentionally recenter my focus on God, I switched off my phone, and just spent quality time with him, entering into an unusual rest. I had renewed strength and felt fortified to go through the process.

"And he said to me, "My grace is sufficient for you, for my strength is made perfect in weakness." 2Corinthians 12:9 (NKJV).

I underwent rigorous preoperative preparation, and the surgery was scheduled to last four hours. The last thing I heard Dr. Smith say was, "I am not going to use a robot; I will have to cut you open because what is there is too big to go through a keyhole. I need to see clearly."

When I woke up, I had a large scar across my abdomen. Dr. Smith came to see me in the postoperative recovery room and said, "The surgery was hard." I wondered what would make a top-notch surgeon say that. "What do you mean?" I asked. "Well, what was left in there was like scar tissue, and it had burst due to the impact of immunotherapy. It had spilled over surrounding organs," he explained. "Thank God we did an open intervention. The immunotherapy had a huge impact, bursting the tumor. We are lucky we opened you up. I was about to close you back up and refer you somewhere else initially, but I decided to go ahead."

Astonished, I reflected on my initial prayer against surgery, realizing God's wisdom and foresight. Sometimes, it seems like God is not listening to us or is letting us go through a hard process that could be shorter, but if you look closely enough, you will find out it is for our good. His thoughts concerning us are good and not evil, to bring us to an expected end.

"For I know the thoughts that I think toward you, says the Lord, thoughts of peace and not of evil, to give you a future and a hope."
Jeremiah 29:11 (NKJV).

"And we know that all things work together for good to those that love God, to those who are the called according to his purpose."
Romans 8:28 (NKJV).

I had a quick recovery even though this phase brought its fair share of trials and discomfort. I was on a temporary ileostomy for four months, which meant my intestine was passed through my stomach while my gut was healing. During that time, I was on a special restricted diet and couldn't eat a lot of things. Eventually, I underwent an ileostomy reversal procedure. I went through the process, but still, I *rose.* God saw me through. I was just a few days out of initial surgery when I turned 41, and I received an all-clear from the doctors to the glory of God. God had done it in his way; *supernatural and spectacular* just depends on how you choose to look at it.

I have learned not to be fixated on the spectacular as I go through life's journey. God's perfect plan unfolds in the supernatural moments of everyday life. When we set a specific outcome and desire it rigidly, it limits our view and causes disappointment. God, the author, is always at work. We may just need to leverage his sufficient grace to go through the process and embrace it. His mercy is abundant, and his plans exceed our expectations. Friends, whether spectacular or supernatural, whether the cup is half full or half empty, remain thankful that you have a cup, and remember that his grace is sufficient.

Principles

1. *The supernatural shows up every day if we look closely enough.*
2. *What the enemy means for evil, God will turn for good.*
3. *Be grateful for the little things while awaiting the big things.*
4. *God will do it however he chooses, do not let another person's spectacular testimony weigh you down, and always focus on your unique journey.*
5. *It may not happen your way, does not mean it won't happen God's way.*
6. *No matter how it looks, all things work together for good for those that love God.*
7. *God may let us go through the process, which may not be our wish, but his grace is sufficient.*
8. *Recenter your focus on the lord don't consider the storm, as this will lead to sinking.*
9. *God sees the bigger picture and will always lead through the best pathway, Trust him.*
10. *Rest in the father; he is always doing the spectacular and supernatural.*

Self-introspection Questions

- *What intentional steps are you taking to recognize and acknowledge supernatural encounters in your life daily? Write down the specific supernatural encounters you have experienced recently, whether big or small.*
- *Do you take inventory of your blessings and intentionally give thanks to God? How can you make gratitude and thanksgiving a more central spiritual practice, fostering a deeper sense of intimacy with God?*
- *Write down all the things bothering you and flip them into gratitude points. With a change of perspective, you will see the supernatural and spectacular in every situation.*

CHAPTER NINE

FRESH OUT OF FIRE

Restoration, Renewal, Rejuvenation

*"Then Nebuchadnezzar was full of fury, and
the expression on his face changed toward
Shadrach, Meshach, and Abednego. He spoke
and commanded that they heat the furnace seven
times more than it was usually heated. And he
commanded certain mighty men of valor who
were in his army to bind Shadrach, Meshach, and
Abednego and cast them into the burning fiery
furnace. Then, these men were bound in their coats,
trousers, turbans, and other garments and were
cast into the midst of the burning fiery furnace.
Therefore, because the king's command was urgent,
and the furnace exceedingly hot, the flame of the
fire killed those men who took Shadrach, Meshach,*

and Abednego. And these three men, Shadrach, Meshach, and Abednego, fell down bound into the midst of the burning fiery furnace. Then King Nebuchadnezzar was astonished and he rose in haste and spoke, saying to his counselors, "Did we not cast three men bound into the midst of the fire? They answered and said. True O king. Look! He answered. I see four men lose. Walking in the midst of the fire. And they are not hurt, and the form of the fourth is like the son of God. Then Nebuchadnezzar went near the mouth of the burning fiery furnace and spoke saying, Shadrach, Meshach, Abednego, servants of the highest God, come out and come here. Then Shadrach, Meshach, and Abednego came from the midst of the fire. And the satraps, administrators, governors, and the king's counselors gathered together, and they saw these men on whose bodies the fire had no power, the hair of their hair was not singed nor were their garments affected, and the smell of fire was not on them."
Daniel 3:19-27 (NKJV)

The song that welled up in my spirit and woke me up that morning was by Nigerian gospel artist Nathaniel Bassey, with lyrics that go, "You've got times and seasons in your hands; you called for light out of darkness." That day, light came out of the darkest season. It seemed like I just regained my sanity; it felt like I had died and risen again. I had gone through the fire but did not smell of smoke because there was a fourth man in the fire. I came out *fresh out of fire* and heard the lord say clearly, "Start to put pen to paper." In obedience, I started to write this book, *Fresh out of Fire: Overcoming a Cancer Journey through Faith in the finished works of Jesus.* When a building crashes and is being rebuilt, the plan, architecture, and everything else are usually not the same; it is made to be better than before, an upgraded version. The uncomfortable thing is that the upgrade will not happen overnight; it will take time, sprinkled with a lot of patience.

I felt like a building that had crashed and was being rebuilt. I was very vulnerable and experienced all sorts of emotions. At some point, it felt like everyone had moved three years ahead while my life had been on pause. As though, my contemporaries had made spiritual, career, and financial progress. However, I realized this perception was untrue. There's no such thing as a pause in the things of the kingdom. My life's journey is not based on comparisons with other people's journeys.

> *"For we dare not class ourselves or compare ourselves with those who commend themselves. But they measuring themselves by themselves and comparing themselves among themselves are not wise."*
> *2 Corinthians 10:12 (NKJV)*

Secondly, I do not own the blueprint of my life; only God does. By whose standard should I measure my progress? The One who created me has the blueprint for my life and is aware of my journey. He alone determines if I am early or late. And guess what? He's got times and seasons in His hands; He restores years.

> *"Yahweh, you alone are my inheritance. You are my prize, my pleasure, and my portion. You hold my destiny and its timing in your hands."*
> *Psalm 16:5 (The passion translation).*

It was very easy to get into a pity party and define my life by this tough season, but I was extremely sure this was just a chapter in the book of my life's journey, not the whole story.

> *And He changes the times and the seasons.*
> *He removes kings and raises up kings; he*
> *gives wisdom to the wise and knowledge*
> *to those who have understanding."*
> *Daniel 2:21 (NKJV).*

To be honest, it wasn't all easy, but the Holy Spirit helped me to crack the code, I anchored myself on praise. I wore my garment of praise, intentionally activated joy, and constantly praised God. I had worship music playing all day. This helped me focus on how far I had come and how far he had brought me.

I had been taught that prayer is like a bank. When we invest time in prayer, it shows up for us when we need it the most. We make withdrawals in seasons when we can't pray, which is often when we need it the most. That's why the Bible says pray without ceasing.

> *"Pray without ceasing."*
> *1 Thessalonians 5:17 (NKJV).*

I saw this play out. The prayers I had made in the past were clearly what I had to draw from in these three years because I couldn't pray as much. Of course, my mother's prayers and the prayers of my tribe also sustained me. During that time, I mostly prayed with my heart, and continuously asked for mercy. In this new season of restoration, I felt like I had overdrawn from my prayer bank, and I needed to refill it. I threw myself into God, tarrying in his presence. God spoke to me in ways I had never experienced before, and I suddenly had clarity about my life's journey and purpose. Everything started to make sense. Although I had to wait months to return to normalcy, every day brought me closer to restoration. God began to restore and renew me beyond what I could imagine.

> *"At the same time that my sanity was restored,*
> *my honor and splendor were returned to me*
> *for the glory of my kingdom. My advisers and*
> *nobles sought me out, and I was restored to my*
> *throne and became even greater than before."*
> *Daniel 4:36 (NIV).*

One day, something happened that marked my heart and my life, catapulting me to a higher level of intimacy with the father. I had an appointment with Dr. Smith. After reviewing my MRI, he decided to schedule me for surgery. He explained the process to me, that it would be a four-hour procedure, after which I would have an ostomy bag on my stomach for three to six months to allow my gut to heal. Hearing this, I was so downcast. I knew this was the treatment protocol, but I didn't want it. At this point, I was exhausted from the entire journey.

That day, I was to travel, so I got on a flight hours later. On the flight, feeling down, I decided to make it a prayer flight since we usually took prayer walks. I had only God to run to. I decided to pray through this news, to cast my cares on him.

> *"Likewise the Spirit also helpeth our infirmities:*
> *for we know not what we should pray for as we*
> *ought: but the Spirit itself maketh intercession for*
> *us with groanings which cannot be uttered."*
> *Romans 8:26 (KJV).*

Throughout the flight, which lasted a couple of hours, I prayed in the spirit. Before then, I had never actually prayed for such a long stretch. This was a new feat for me. Then something happened, by the time we were almost landing there was a shift. It was as if I was being carried and I felt light. I hit the gusher! Friend, there are deeper depths, dimensions, and higher heights in God. That day unlocked something brand new in my prayer life. Though I felt lost in the wilderness, it was there I found a new dimension of his presence. This experience became a vehicle of intimacy, ushering me into the throne room. The wilderness gave me a friend.

The miracles that followed blew my mind. I started to seek his face, desiring to press into his presence more and more. There was just something incredible about hitting the gusher, a place of intense communion and fellowship with the father. It was amazing. I realized that there is always more, I had found a treasure, stepping into something new. Emerging fresh out of the fire, I entered a new dimension with a fresh supply of grace to continue to seek him in a new way. I encountered Jehovah Rapha, God my healer, and El-Roi, the God that sees me. I had tasted of his mercy.

"Oh, taste and see that the lord is good;
blessed is the man who trusts in him."
Psalm 34:8 (NKJV).

The Holy Spirit guided me in navigating new levels of intimacy with Him, which is the essence of continuous renewal and transformation. We often think that restoration is in only physical things like money and a career, but to God, the most important restoration is that of our soul.

"He restores my soul; he leads me in the paths
of righteousness, for his name's sake."
Psalm 23:3 (NKJV).

"For what will it profit a man if he gains the
whole world, and loses his own soul?"
Mark 8:36 (NKJV).

Our soul is more important to God, and eventually, the physical and material things will be added to us. All other forms of prosperity happen in direct proportion to the prosperity of our soul.

"Beloved, I pray that you may prosper in all things
and be in health, just as your soul prospers."
3 John 1:2(NKJV).

I tapped into new dimensions and had come full circle. Everything about my journey and purpose started to make sense. I had clarity like never before, and all the things God had told me in the past began to consolidate. I understood what Job meant when he said:

"I have heard of you by the hearing of
the ear, but now my eye sees you."
Job 42:5 (NKJV).

As I sought intimacy with the Lord, He revealed himself as Ebenezer, my stone of help. This gave me a new perspective: restoration, renewal, and rejuvenation are all by-products of an ongoing relationship with the father, allowing him to shape us into the extraordinary. I embarked on this journey desperately, having seen the lord, the power of the cross, and encountering Jesus in a new way. Renewal came by immersing myself in the word, pressing in and reaching new heights in him. God uses our challenges to refine and bring beauty out of ashes, turning those ashes into a foundation for something greater working all things together for good.

"And we know that all things work together for our good to those who love God, to those who are the called according to his purpose."
Romans 8:28 (NKJV).

Every day unveils a new version of me I never thought was possible. I strive to become more aligned with him daily, renewed through his word and the embrace of his presence. He is my everything, my treasure. If this fresh perspective and understanding of the father was all I gained from this journey, I'm forever grateful. I have become much better than before, experiencing a holistic renewal in my spirit, soul, and body. I didn't come out of that season the same; it changed me. He gave me a new name, and I've found beauty in him and a communion that surpasses my wildest expectations.

"Then the spirit of the lord will come upon you, and you will prophesy with them and be turned into another man."
1 Sam 10:6 (NKJV).

"Now The Lord blessed the latter days of Job's life more than the beginning."
(Job 42:12a (NKJV).

In this world, we may face tough wilderness experiences and hard terrains, often marked by challenges that do not respect religious affiliations or records of good deeds. These challenges are often beyond us, sometimes leaving us with worries that make us feel like the weight of the world is on our shoulders. Other times, it's shame that we can't comprehend, rejection that seems totally unfair, or disappointment that defies all strategy. We encounter closed doors that mercilessly remain locked no matter how hard we push, and, of course, the unexplainable pain of waiting and the helplessness that comes with it. But one thing is sure: if we lean on God, the fire births something fresh; a hope, a reward, a purpose, His presence.

Nothing beats a life that pauses to thank God. I thank him daily for both the little and big things. I find God in every single detail and no longer take many things for granted. From being able to make meals for my family to sleeping on a bed - I slept on a massage chair for almost a year because the bed hurt so bad. I didn't even know the clothes my kids had in their wardrobe for years. The journey was challenging, but I'm reminded of the greatest power and humbled knowing that I'm no better than those who faced similar struggles and whose journey ended differently. It's solely the mercy of God.

Another humbling fact is, that even if my story had not ended this way, to the glory of his name, it wouldn't change the fact that he is God. He remains God, self-sufficient and unchanging, regardless. I am forever grateful for the finished works of Jesus and that he did not leave me without a helper - the spirit of truth to guide me into all truth. In this season, I learned to be a person who inquires, listens to the father, and gets clear instructions on the *when's, how's, and where's.*

"So David inquired of the lord, saying, shall I pursue after this troop? Shall I overtake them?

And he answered him, pursue: for thou shalt surely overtake them, and without fail to recover all."
1 Samuel 30:8(NKJV).

I have intentionally built altars of praise to represent and mark this defining part of my life's journey. I reiterate that my anchor through this season of restoration has been joy and patience. I chose how I waited. I had to wait in between surgeries, getting back to work, and settling into my life. I uncovered God's word afresh like never before, unlearning and relearning him, spending quality time in his presence. This was a choice I made – to embrace restoration, renewal, and revival by the Holy Spirit. Restoration is not a destination; it's a continuous journey.

Challenges and experiences will occur as long as we are on earth, but these wilderness experiences can typically do one of two things: make you bitter or better. The choice is yours. The outcome depends on who you run to and what you anchor on. I recommend Jesus.

Dr Creflo Dollar puts it beautifully in his Thanksgiving video on YouTube (you should check that out). "I have another chance at life, and I want to live it. I'm in better shape than I have ever been in my life. This is the greatest power!" He said.

"For surely there is an end, and thine expectation shall not be cut off."
Prov 23:18 (NKJV).

Principles

1. *You may go through the fire but will not be consumed if you have faith in God.*

2. *God always restores to better than before.*
3. *During restoration, anchor yourself on praise and joy.*
4. *Do not compare yourself with others, he who has called you has your timing in his hands.*
5. *Friend, Invest time in prayers, log in hours in prayers.*
6. *Throw yourself into the father, he will bring you to a new level of intimacy.*
7. *He is a restorer, no matter what you feel you have lost.*
8. *Be patient with yourself restoration is not an event or destination; it is a continuous journey.*
9. *Choose to spend time in his presence, where transformation, renewal, and rejuvenation come from.*
10. *If you lean on him, you will emerge better than you have ever been.*

Self-introspection Questions

- *What specific practices or activities bring you joy and peace amongst challenges? How do you cultivate joy and patience during your restoration season?*
- *Do you spend quality time in prayer, and the word? Identify areas that can be better. And ask the Holy Spirit to help you as you come out renewed, restored and fresh out of fire.*
- *How do you respond to setbacks or obstacles? Do you trust in God's faithfulness to see you through? Do you know that challenges are opportunities for refinement and transformation?*

CHAPTER TEN

PURPOSE ON THE OTHER SIDE OF PAIN

I have many scars - from those etched on my body to those imprinted on my soul. Each scar tells a story of trials, tribulations, and triumphs. Among these scars is what looks like the sign of the cross, a long line across my belly, and another along its side. I am proud of my scars as they are victory signs. They are evidence that I went to war, and somebody fought for me - His name is Jesus. As the songwriter says, "The number of my scars are the number of my victories." My scars bear witness that the cross is still potent in its power, the cross still oozes power, there is still balm in Gilead and Jehovah Rapha is still a healer.

"From now on, let no man trouble me; for I bear in my body the marks of the Lord Jesus Christ." Galatians 6:17 (NKJV).

The view on the other side of pain is different. As God recalibrates and refocuses, purpose emerges, making the pain worthwhile. I've been changed by the challenges I have overcome with God's help. The journey has molded me in many ways, into someone more empathetic and, most importantly, helped me see life beyond myself. I've made a conscious decision to share my story and lay bare my scars in obedience, with the hope that if just one person has their faith lifted and can overcome a challenging season by drawing strength from my journey, then my pain will not go to waste. It indeed has a purpose.

> **"Who comforts us in all our tribulation that we may be able to comfort those who are in any trouble, with the comfort with which we ourselves are comforted by God."**
> **2 Corinthians 1:4 (NKJV).**

One of the many profound things that this journey birthed was a connection between my current experience and an event over a decade ago. After graduating from medical school, I went through a medical internship, and one of my rotations was to the pediatric oncology department. There, I had a patient called 'Sanumi,' which means God have mercy on me in Yoruba language, the Nigerian tribe I hail from. He was diagnosed with cancer at ten years old and for some reason, he had a special connection with me, always insisting that I administer his treatment. This was quite hard because I was pregnant, and his treatments posed some risks to me. To calm him, we always had a plan on the team where I'd give him a placebo(not the real medication) - most times just water for injection – and then my colleague would come right after and give the real treatment. This was our daily routine. Sanumi's journey drained me emotionally. I witnessed the struggle his parents faced as they could hardly pay for his treatment, and the family was very impacted.

What was worse was we had cases of other mothers on the ward abandoning their kids as they could no longer bear the financial burden. They would literarily run away. One way we mitigated this was by writing off some of their hospital bills through a fund operated by a Nigerian philanthropist. I saw these mothers jump for joy when we told them part of their pending bills had been written off by the fund.

We eventually lost Sanumi, mainly due to his family's insufficient finances. This broke my heart. I remember discussing with my husband, telling him I would like to come back in the future to set up such a fund to help families dealing with chronic illnesses. I completed my internship soon after, but I got caught up with life and completely forgot about that promise. Fast forward to after my own cancer journey - I had come full circle, and the Holy Spirit reminded me of this encounter I had over a decade ago. I knew it was time. This led to my creating a fund, an initiative through my nonprofit, oyster care foundation, which helps fund cancer treatment in children like Sanumi in Africa. Having walked in their shoes and experienced something similar, I could relate to how hard their cancer journey is, not to mention the additional layer of financial constraint. The cost of cancer treatment is a whole different conversation, and I knew I had to ease that burden.

As far as my journey goes, one thing that distinctly marks it is the realization that without God's help and mercy, the kind of medical treatment I received would have been beyond reach. Without a health insurance company covering hundreds of thousands of dollars in bills for me, it would have been impossible - a privilege not everyone has. I understood mercy spoke for me. Not everyone is fortunate to live in a society where they have health insurance companies supporting the bills. I am grateful for the privilege I now have in funding hospital bills for children like Sanumi living with cancer and easing their journeys, ministering Christ's love in practical ways.

God, in his sovereignty, turns our trials into purpose. This is just one of the many experiences where I have witnessed how purpose has been birthed out of my pain. God is not unaware of our struggles. My unique journey holds lessons for all, serving as a testament that even in the darkest moments, purpose can be illuminated. Let my story inspire you to find purpose in your pain. Trust that God can birth something beautiful, something bigger than you that serves humanity, even out of the most challenging circumstances.

I share this not just as a personal tale but as an encouragement for those going through diverse journeys. Regardless of the challenges, if you circle back to God, refocus, and center on him, you will find purpose in pain. It's about living beyond ourselves and understanding that he has an agenda. God is working, recalibrating, and birthing something beautiful out of the painful and challenging situations. This perspective makes pain look really small when viewed from the lens of purpose. Indeed, purpose sits on the other side of pain.

> *"And we know that all things work together*
> *for good to those who love God, to those who*
> *are the called according to his purpose."*
> *Romans 8:28 (NKJV).*

My last and final appointment with Dr. Smith marked the end of the entire journey. This was two years after being diagnosed and four years since the onset of symptoms. He looked at me and said, "To be honest, yours is a big win because that tumor was too large. I am so glad we got to see the end of this!" he added. As a doctor, I understood those words in depth. What he meant was clear- this was nothing short of a miracle! I have overcome and emerged stronger from cancer through faith in the finished works of Jesus. Friend, faith is indeed the believer's voice of victory. If you look close enough at the cross of calvary, you will see a little girl ...that's me right there, hiding right behind the cross. It's a finished work!.

> **"Yet in all these things, we are more than conquerors
> and gain an overwhelming victory through
> him who loved us (so much he died for us)."
> Romans 8:37 (Amplified version).**

Principles

1. *Whatever your scars look like, they are victory signs.*
2. *When your scars begin to form, you have a victory story to tell.*
3. *There is still balm in Gilead, the cross still oozes power.*
4. *When we lay bare our scars, we help others heal.*
5. *When God is in it, it will make sense at the end.*
6. *You have to look beyond yourself but unto God to find purpose in pain.*
7. *God can use us in the same area where we face a challenge.*
8. *Despite the pain, recenter, and refocus on God.*
9. *Flip the pain into purpose, victory is sure.*
10. *All things, including the painful challenges we face work together for good if you place it in God's hands.*

Self-introspection Questions

- *Journal about the emotional and physical scars and experiences that have marked your heart?*

- *Have you taken time to place your scars and tough journeys in God's hands, knowing that in the hands of the lord they become signs of victory?*

- *What steps can you take to live out the decision to hide yourself behind the cross, allowing God to write a new story of purpose in your life? Do you believe that all things are working together for your good, even in the midst of trials and challenges?*

SALVATION PRAYER

My story woven into the fabric of Dr. Creflo Dollars journey is a testament to the universal power of God's grace. Age, gender, generation, culture, popularity, strata, none of this matter when it comes to the boundless grace available through the finished works of Jesus, which is the greatest power.

Dr. Dollar may be older, male, an American, a well-known popular televangelist, in contrast, I am younger, female, proudly Nigerian of African descent, an ordinary girl.

But here is the beauty of it; God's grace doesn't discriminate based on gender, culture, age, pedigree, generation, or even financial status. It's solely about the grace and mercy of God and what Jesus accomplished for us ALL on the cross. It is FREE! And available to All!

"There is neither Jew nor Greek, there is
neither slave nor free, there is neither male
nor female, for you are all one in Christ Jesus,
and if you are Christ, then you are Abraham's
seed, and heirs according to the promise."
Galatians 3: 28-29 (NKJV).

So, I extend to you today the invitation to salvation. It doesn't matter if you've read this book and are not a Christian or if you are hearing about giving your life to Jesus for the first time. If you say this prayer and genuinely believe in your heart. And accept Jesus in your heart, you join the kingdom tribe that experience God in multifaceted ways-Jehovah El Shammah, El Roi, the God who sees and guides.

Your entire story changes because the Holy Spirit comes into your life, marking your journey with grace, purpose, and divine touch that transcends all human distinctions. So, my dear friend, join the train of those who have embraced this finished work, and let your story be transformed by the unfathomable love of God.

SAY THIS PRAYER:

DEAR LORD JESUS, I KNOW THAT I AM A SINNER. I ASK FOR YOUR FORGIVENESS. I BELIEVE YOU DIED FOR MY SINS AND ROSE FROM THE DEAD. I TURN FROM MY SINS AND INVITE YOU TO COME INTO MY HEART AND LIFE. I RECEIVE YOU INTO MY HEART, AND I TRUST AND FOLLOW YOU AS MY LORD AND SAVIOUR. IN JESUS NAME I PRAY, AMEN!

Welcome home!!

Next steps

Get plugged into a bible believing church, I would recommend;

- World changers church international- @worldchangerschurch
- God's love tabernacle church international @Gltchurch
- Covenant nation – @covenantccentre
- Koinonia global @koinonia.abuja

Check them out on all social media platforms (Facebook, Instagram, YouTube, etc.)

APPENDIX

HEALING DECLARATIONS.

Why healing declarations?

Throughout my journey, one thing I constantly did was to take my confessions and declarations. Regardless of the challenges I faced, whether it was daunting doctors' reports or discouraging scan results, the enemy persistently hurled negative thoughts my way. However, I had learnt that the way to resist the devil is by speaking the word of God. Which means not just pondering God's word internally but speaking it into existence, manifesting its truth in my life.

"Let us hold fast to the confession of our hope without wavering, because who has promised is faithful."
Hebrews 10:23 (NKJV).

God created the world with words; the act of declaring and confessing God's word is not merely a suggestion but a fundamental principle in the kingdom of God. The word of God is alive and active, and through our declarations, we participate in the creative process ordained by God himself.

Even in moments of doubt or apparent silence be rest assured that your declarations are not in vain. Every time you speak and decree God's word in faith, things happen in the spirit, and divine order is established.

"Thou shalt also decree a thing, and it shall be established unto thee: And the light shall shine upon thy ways."
Job 22:28 (KJV).

In crafting these declarations, my aim is to provide you with a springboard to ignite your journey of declaration. Yet, more importantly is for you to delve into God's word personally, allowing the Holy Spirit to illuminate scriptures that speak to your unique circumstances. I encourage you to take your time to make your personal declarations by the guidance of the Holy Spirit and write them down.

For additional support, the "Fresh out of fire journal" is readily available for FREE download on our website and in hardcopy format.

By committing your declarations to writing, you reinforce the presence in your heart and empower yourself to declare them consistently with the help of the Holy Spirit. Always remember, the word of faith we speak is our voice of victory! Speak life!

"Death and life are in the power of the tongue: and those who love it will eat its fruit."
Proverbs 18:21 (NKJV).

I DECREE AND DECLARE MY DWELLING.

I declare that I dwell in the secret of the most high, I abide under the shadow of the Almighty (Psalm 91:1).

I declare that the lord is my refuge and my fortress. My God in him I trust (Psalm 91:2).

I declare that surely; I am delivered from the snare of the fowler and from the perilous pestilence. God covers me under his feathers, and I take refuge under his wings! The truth of God's word is my shield and buckler (Psalm 91:3-4).

I declare that the lord has chosen me; he has desired me as his dwelling forever (Psalm 132:13-14).

I declare that goodness and mercy shall follow me all the days of my life, and I shall dwell in the house of the Lord forever (Psalm 23:6).

I declare that God is my hiding place, and he protects me from trouble and surrounds me with songs of deliverance (Psalm 32:7).

I declare that I dwell in the house of the Lord all the days of my life, I gaze on the beauty of the lord and seek him in his temple (Psalm 27:4).

I declare that you are my refuge and my shield, I put my hope in your word (Psalm 119:114).

I DECREE AND DECLARE GODS LOVE FOR ME.

I decree and declare that I am persuaded that neither death nor life, nor angels nor rulers, nor things present nor things to come, nor powers, nor height nor depth, nor anything else in all creation, will be able to separate me from that love of God in Christ Jesus our lord (Romans 8:38-39).

I declare that God loves me so much that he laid his life down for me (John 15:13).

I declare that God so loved me that he gave his only son for me; I believe in him, and therefore I will not perish, but I will have everlasting life (John 3:16).

I declare that God has loved me with everlasting love, and he has continued in his faithfulness to me (Jeremiah 31:3).

I declare that God loves me immensely, that while I was yet a sinner, he died for me (Romans 5:8).

I declare that I am loved by God! He first loved me and sent his only son as an atoning sacrifice for my sins (1 John 4:10).

I decree that though the mountains be shaken, and the hills be removed, yet God's unfailing love for me will not be shaken nor his covenant of peace be removed (Isiah 54:10).

I DECREE AND DECLARE FAITH OVER FEAR.

I declare that I shall not be afraid of the terror by night, nor of the arrow that flies by day. I do not fear the pestilence that walks in darkness, nor the destruction that lays waste at noonday (Psalm 91:5-6).

I declare that I do not fear for God is with me, I am not dismayed, for he is my God. He strengthens me and helps me and upholds me with his righteous right hand (Isaiah 41:10).

I declare that I have faith, and I ask God to heal me in faith, with no doubts, I am not tossed to and fro like the wind (James 1:6).

I declare that I have faith, and I therefore please God. I come to God believing that he is and he is a rewarder of those that diligently seek him (Hebrews 11:6).

I declare that nothing is impossible with God (Luke 1:37).

I declare that I walk by faith and not by sight (Romans 10:17).

I declare that I am born of God, and I overcome the world, I decree that this is the victory that overcomes the world, even my faith (1 John 5:4).

I declare that I hold fast to the confession of my faith without wavering, for he who promised is faithful (Hebrews 10:23).

I DECREE AND DECLARE THE FINISHED WORKS OF JESUS.

I declare that I have been crucified with Christ, and I no longer live, but Christ lives in me. The life I now live in this body, I live by faith in the son of God, who loved me and gave himself for me (Galatians 2:20).

I declare that he was wounded for our transgressions, He was bruised for my iniquities, the chastisement of my peace was laid upon him, by his stripes I was healed (Isiah 53:5).

I declare that he bore my sins in his body on a tree, that I having died to sins, might live for righteousness, by whose stripes I was healed (1 Peter 2:24).

I declare that my healing is a finished work. Jesus died, and the cross that because of the substitutional sacrifice. It is finished. My healing is a done deal (John 19:30).

I declare that Christ is the mediator of the new covenant that those who are called may receive the promised eternal inheritance. He has died as a ransom to set me free from the sins committed under the first covenant (Hebrews 9:15).

I declare that all things are of God, who has reconciled us to himself through Jesus Christ, and has given us the ministry of reconciliation. I decree that God has reconciled me to himself, not imputing my trespasses to me, and has committed to me the word of reconciliation (2 Corinthians 5:18).

I DECREE AND DECLARE THAT I OVERCOME.

I declare that a thousand shall fall at my side, ten thousand at my right hand, but it shall not come near me (Psalm 91:7)

I declare that no evil shall befall me, nor shall any plague come near my dwelling, the angels of the lord take charge over me, they keep me in all my ways (Psalm 91:11).

I declare that I call upon the lord, and he answers me, he is with me in trouble; I am delivered, and satisfied with long life (Psalm 91:15-16).

I declare that in all these things, I am more than a conqueror through him who loved me (Romans 8:28).

I declare that I overcame by the blood of the lamb, and by the word of my testimony, and I love my life unto death (Revelation 12:11).

I declare that I overcome because he that is in me is greater than he who is the world (I John 4:4).

I declare that I overcome because I believe that Jesus is the son of God (1 John 5:5).

I declare that though I pass through the waters, He is with me, and when I pass through the rivers, they will not overflow me; when I walk through the fire, I shall not be burned, nor shall the flame scorch me (Isiah 43:2).

I DECLARE ALL THINGS ARE WORKING OUT FOR MY GOOD.

I declare that God's plan for my life is good and perfect, to prosper me and not to harm me, to give me a future and hope (Jeremiah 29:11).

I declare that all things work together for my good because I love him, and I am called according to his purpose (Romans 8:28).

I declare that I prosper, and I am in health, even as my soul prospers (3 John 1:2).

I declare that he has begun a good work in me will bring it to completion at the day of Jesus Christ (Philippians 1:6).

I declare that before I was formed in the womb, God knew me, he knew my journey, he set me apart and appointed me as a prophet to the nations (Jeremiah 1:5).

I DECREE AND DECLARE GODS MERCY.

I declare that goodness and mercy shall follow me all the days of my life, and I shall dwell in the house of the Lord forever (Psalm 23:6).

I declare that the mercies of God never come to an end, they are new every morning, great is thy faithfulness (Lamentations 3:22-23).

I declare that I draw near to the throne of grace, and I receive mercy and find grace to help in the time of need (Hebrews 4:16).

I declare that God's mercy triumphs over judgement (James 2:13).

I declare that I come boldly to the throne of grace, that I may obtain mercy and find grace to help in the time of need (Hebrews 4:16).

I DECLARE STRENGTH AND WHOLENESS.

I declare that though my flesh and my heart may fail, God is the strength of my heart and my portion forever (Psalm 73:26).

I declare that the Lord is gracious to me; I long for him. The Lord is my strength every morning, my salvation in times of distress (Isiah 33:2).

I declare that I am comforted in affliction; his words have given me life (Psalm 119:50).

I declare that as my days are, so shall my strength be (Deuteronomy 33:25).

I declare that I pay attention to God's word and incline my ear to his sayings. I do not let them depart from my eyes, I keep them in the midst of my heart, for they are life to those that find them and health to all their flesh (Proverbs 4:20-22).

I declare Lord, that you heal me, and I am healed. You save me, and I will be saved (Jeremiah 17:14).

I declare that he has given me strength when I am weary and increased my power when I am weak (Isiah 40:29).

I declare that I have called to God for help, and he healed me (Psalm 30:2).

I declare that as I wait upon the lord, he renews my strength. I soar on wings like eagles, I will run and not go weary, I will walk and will not faint (Isiah 40:31).

I DECREE AND DECLARE RESTORATION.

I declare that I am restored from my sickbed and I am restored from the bed of illness (Psalm 41:3).

I declare that though I walk through the valley of the shadow of death, I will fear no evil, for God is with me, his rod and his staff; comfort me (Psalm 23:4).

I declare that the lord restores me to health and heals my wounds (Jeremiah 30:17).

I declare that the years that the locust hath eaten, the cankerworm and caterpillar are restored to me (Joel 2:25).

I declare that I receive from the lord twice as much as I had before (Job 42:5).

I DECLARE THANKSGIVING AND REJOICING

I declare that I enter his gate with thanksgiving I make a joyful noise to him with songs of praise (Psalm 95:2).

I give thanks to God in all circumstances, for this is the will of God in Christ Jesus for me (1 Thessalonians 5:18).

I declare that I am not anxious about anything, but in everything by prayer and supplication with thanksgiving, I let my request be made known to God (Phillipians 4:6).

I declare that my soul blesses the lord and I do not forget his benefits; he forgives my iniquity, he heals my diseases, he redeems my life from the pit, he crowns me with steadfast love and mercy, he satisfies me with good so that my youth is renewed like an eagle (Psalm 103:2-5).

I declare that I give thanks to the lord with my whole heart; I recount all of his wonderful deeds (Psalm 9:1).

I declare that I give the lord thanks due to his righteousness, and I will sing praises to the name of the lord, most high (Psalm 7:17).

I declare that I give thanks to the Lord, I call upon his name and make known his deeds among the people (1 Chronicles 16:8).

I declare that I always rejoice (I Thessalonians 5:16).

I declare that I enter his gates with thanksgiving and his courts with praise; I give thanks to him and praise his name (Psalm 100:4).

I declare that I will praise the name of God with a song, I will magnify him with thanksgiving (Psalm 69:30).

Printed in the United States
by Baker & Taylor Publisher Services